Kenya:

Malaria Operational Plan FY 2014

Table of Contents

ABBREVIATIONS 3

EXECUTIVE SUMMARY 4

STRATEGY 7

President's Malaria Initiative 7

Malaria Situation in Kenya 7

Health System Delivery Structure and Ministry of Health Organization 9

Country Malaria Control Strategy 11

Kenya Malaria Control Strategy – strategic approach by intervention 12

Integration, Collaboration and Coordination 14

PMI Goals, Targets and Indicators 15

Progress on Coverage/Impact Indicators to Date 15

Challenges, Opportunities and Threats 16

PMI Support Strategy 18

OPERATIONAL PLAN 19

Indoor Residual Spraying 19

Insecticide-Treated Nets 22

Malaria in Pregnancy (MIP) 26

Case Management 28

    DIAGNOSIS 28

    TREATMENT 31

    PHARMACEUTICAL MANAGEMENT 35

Monitoring & Evaluation 37

Behavior Change Communication 42

Capacity Building and Health Systems Strengthening 45

Staffing & Administration 47

Table 1: Year 7 (FY 2014) Budget Breakdown by Partner 50

Table 2: FY 2014 Planned Obligations Kenya 52

ABBREVIATIONS

ACT	Artemisinin-based combination therapy
ANC	Antenatal care
AL	Artemether-lumefantrine
BCC	Behavior change communication
CDC	Centers for Disease Control and Prevention
CHEW	Community Health Extension Workers
CHW	Community health workers
DFID	Department for International Development (UK)
DHS	Demographic and Health Survey
DHIS2	District Health Information System
DOMC	Division of Malaria Control
FELTP	Field Epidemiology and Laboratory Training Program
GHI	Global Health Initiative
Global Fund	The Global Fund for HIV/AIDS, Tuberculosis and Malaria
GoK	Government of Kenya
IEC	Information, education and communication
IPTp	Intermittent preventive treatment for pregnant women
IRS	Indoor residual spraying
ITN	Insecticide-treated net
KEMSA	Kenya Medical Supplies Authority
M&E	Monitoring and evaluation
MIP	Malaria in pregnancy
MIS	Malaria Indicator Survey
NMS	National Malaria Strategy
PEPFAR	President's Emergency Plan for AIDS Relief
PMI	President's Malaria Initiative
RDT	Rapid diagnostic test
SP	Sulfadoxine-pyrimethamine
USAID	United States Agency for International Development
WHO	World Health Organization

EXECUTIVE SUMMARY

Malaria prevention and control is a major foreign assistance objective of the U.S. Government. In May 2009, President Barack Obama announced the Global Health Initiative (GHI), a comprehensive effort to reduce the burden of disease and promote healthy communities and families around the world. Through the GHI, the US Government will improve health outcomes, building upon and expanding successes in addressing specific diseases and issues. The President's Malaria Initiative (PMI) is a core component of the GHI, along with HIV/AIDS, maternal and child health, and tuberculosis. PMI was launched in June 2005 as a five-year, $1.2 billion initiative to rapidly scale up malaria prevention and treatment interventions and reduce malaria-related mortality by 50% in 15 high-burden countries in sub-Saharan Africa. With passage of the 2008 Lantos-Hyde Act, funding for PMI has now been extended through FY 2014.

A decline in the burden of malaria in Kenya has been observed in recent years due to aggressive efforts to scale up malaria control measures. This has reduced malaria transmission intensity in most parts of the country. In spite of this, moderate to high levels of transmission persist in certain endemic zones and the 2010 Kenya Malaria Indicator Survey (MIS) confirmed that malaria prevalence remains more than twice as high in rural areas (12%) than in urban areas (5%). Malaria prevalence around Lake Victoria is particularly high at 38%, while prevalence in other epidemiological zones has dropped to less than 5%. Consequently, as part of Kenya's National Malaria Strategy 2009–2017 (NMS), prevention and control interventions are tailored to the current epidemiology of malaria, with efforts concentrated in the lake-endemic zone.

Kenya has a Round 10 Malaria grant from the Global Fund to Fight AIDS, Tuberculosis and Malaria (Global Fund), which was signed in early 2012 and has a Phase 1 (September 2011– December 2013) value of over $38 million. Phase 2 is currently being negotiated. The grant provides critical support for maintaining universal coverage of insecticide-treated nets (ITNs), ensuring a nationwide supply of artemisinin-based combination therapies (ACTs), and implementing the national diagnostic policy to provide malaria rapid diagnostic tests (RDTs) to all health facilities. The funding does not fully cover commodity and programmatic needs, and Kenya relies on external partners to help ensure effective implementation of malaria prevention and control activities. The activities that PMI is proposing for FY 2014 are matched with identified needs and priorities described in the NMS and build on investments designed to improve and expand malaria-related services during the first five years of PMI funding. The proposed FY 2014 PMI budget for Kenya is $32.4 million.

To achieve the goals and targets of Kenya's Division of Malaria Control (DOMC) and PMI, the following major activities will be supported with FY 2014 funding:

Indoor residual spraying (IRS): PMI has supported the national IRS program since 2008. PMI protected over 2.4 million people in 2012 (reaching 98% of the targeted households) and currently targets priority areas in three counties in the Lake Victoria endemic region. In 2014, Kenya's IRS program will transition to a non-pyrethroid insecticide, a change rendered necessary by the emergence of insecticide resistance throughout much of western Kenya. The use of a more expensive non-pyrethroid insecticide will increase the cost of IRS. Furthermore, the shorter duration of residual activity of this insecticide may necessitate two rounds of spraying per year rather than one. With FY 2014 funding, PMI will continue to support IRS in up to three priority counties in collaboration with the DOMC and the United Kingdom's Department for International Development (DFID). The estimated population coverage will be almost 2 million people living in 555,473 households. PMI will support entomological monitoring to detect insecticide resistance and measure mosquito populations in counties transitioning away from IRS programs, as well as in counties with ongoing IRS programs.

Insecticide-treated nets: Kenya seeks to achieve universal ITN coverage, defined as one net per two people, within endemic and epidemic-prone counties. In 2011–2012, Kenya conducted a rolling mass campaign to reach universal coverage of ITNs in priority endemic areas; more than 11 million ITNs were distributed in Nyanza, Western, Rift Valley and Coast Provinces. Other distribution strategies include free or highly-subsidized ITNs provided through antenatal care (ANC) and child health clinics, child health action days, community-based initiatives, and retail outlets. The 2010 MIS showed that household ownership of ITNs was 48%, while the proportions of children under five years of age and pregnant women who slept under an ITN the previous night were 42% and 41%, respectively. PMI will purchase an estimated 1.7 million more ITNs by the end of 2013.

To continue supporting national ITN policies, PMI will procure an estimated 1.8 million ITNs with FY 2014 funding to support free routine distribution through ANC clinics and the planned 2014–2015 mass campaign. PMI will support the DOMC to continue development of innovative ways to replace worn-out nets at the community level. Additionally, PMI will continue to work with non-governmental organizations on community-based behavior change communication programs to increase demand for ITNs and encourage correct and consistent use.

Intermittent preventive treatment of pregnant women (IPTp): The 2010 MIS showed improved coverage of IPTp; however, only 25% of pregnant women receive two or more doses of sulfadoxine-pyrimethamine, despite high ANC clinic attendance (i.e. 86% of women attend ANC two or more times during their pregnancies). With FY 2014 funding, PMI will support the scale up of IPTp in two counties targeting over 2,000 facility-based health care workers and about 4,000 community health workers to ensure increased uptake of IPTp. In addition, PMI will continue to support IPTp interventions in all malaria endemic areas.

Case management: The most recent edition of the National Guidelines for Diagnosis, Treatment and Prevention of Malaria in Kenya was issued in 2010 and recommends diagnosis-based treatment as part of effective case management. By the end of 2013, PMI will have procured over 4.5 million RDTs in support of rolling out the DOMC's diagnostic policy to use RDTs in all dispensaries and health centers. By the end of 2013, PMI will have also procured an estimated 3.5 million treatments of the ACT, artemether-lumefantrine (AL). With FY 2014 funding, PMI will procure an estimated 3.75 million RDTs to support the continued national roll-out and community case management strategy. PMI will also support training and supervision to strengthen malaria diagnostics use at county and facility levels through implementation of quality assurance systems. Additionally, PMI will procure approximately 4.8 million AL treatment regimens to help ensure an adequate supply of ACTs throughout the year. PMI will also continue strengthening the supply chain and logistics systems to ensure reliable access and a steady supply of essential commodities to the facility level. To ensure that AL is properly prescribed in accordance with national guidelines and to improve the quality of malaria case management, PMI will help strengthen and support health worker supervision systems.

Behavior change communication (BCC): Through community mobilization, interpersonal communication, use of mass media, and local radio stations to disseminate key messages and encourage positive health-seeking behavior, PMI is promoting increased ITN use, prompt diagnosis and treatment for fever, and demand for IPTp in prioritized counties. With FY 2014 funding, PMI will continue to support cross-cutting BCC investments at community, county, and national levels, with a particular emphasis on strengthening community-based communication activities.

Monitoring and evaluation (M&E): PMI provides support to the DOMC to ensure that critical gaps in the Kenya Malaria Monitoring and Evaluation Plan 2009–2017 are filled. In the past, PMI has supported the development and roll out of the national surveillance plan, an assessment of the implementation of the epidemic preparedness and response plan, epidemiologic surveillance in IRS areas, and epidemiology training and activities to standardize malaria data collection and reporting. With FY 2014 funds, PMI will continue efforts to increase the DOMC's M&E capacity to analyze data and conduct ongoing program monitoring for specific interventions. The areas of support include: malaria surveillance in all epidemiological zones, including epidemic-prone counties; monitoring quality of care for malaria case management; strengthening timely commodity reporting; continued *in vivo* antimalarial drug efficacy monitoring, and the collection of malaria information at the health facility level through the District Health Information System.

Health Systems Strengthening and Integration: PMI has invested in efforts to build capacity and integrate across programs. PMI/Kenya strengthens the overall health system by improving governance in the pharmaceutical sector, strengthening pharmaceutical management systems, expanding access to essential medicines, and improving service delivery in the different intervention areas. In 2013, PMI supported the transition to the district health information system for monitoring of malaria commodities along with routine malaria indicator data. PMI also supported the training of ten DOMC staff in senior management and leadership, and another 13 staff were trained on the basics of quantitative and qualitative data analysis. With FY 2014 funds, PMI will continue to build human resource capacity by training healthcare personnel and improve health service delivery by strengthening systems.

STRATEGY

President's Malaria Initiative

Malaria prevention and control is a major foreign assistance objective of the U.S. Government. In May 2009, President Barack Obama announced the Global Health Initiative (GHI), a comprehensive effort to reduce the burden of disease and promote healthy communities and families around the world. Through the GHI, the United States will help partner countries improve health outcomes, building upon and expanding the US Government's successes in addressing specific diseases and issues.

The President's Malaria Initiative (PMI) is a core component of the GHI, along with HIV/AIDS, maternal and child health, and tuberculosis. PMI was launched in June 2005 as a five-year, $1.2 billion initiative to rapidly scale up malaria prevention and treatment interventions and reduce malaria-related mortality by 50% in 15 high-burden countries in sub-Saharan Africa. With passage of the 2008 Lantos-Hyde Act, funding for PMI was extended through FY 2014, and as part of the GHI, the goal of PMI is to achieve a 70% reduction in the burden of malaria in the original 15 countries by 2015. This will be achieved by reaching 85% coverage of the most vulnerable groups — children under five years of age and pregnant women — with proven preventive and therapeutic interventions, including artemisinin-based combination therapies (ACTs), insecticide-treated nets (ITNs), intermittent preventive treatment for pregnant women (IPTp), and indoor residual spraying (IRS).

Kenya was selected as a PMI country in FY 2007. Large-scale implementation of ITNs, ACTs and IPTp began in FY 2008 and has progressed rapidly with support from PMI and other partners. The FY 2014 Malaria Operational Plan presents a detailed implementation plan for Kenya, based on the PMI Multi-Year Strategy and Plan and the Kenya National Malaria Strategy 2009–2017 (NMS). The Malaria Operational Plan was developed in consultation with the Division of Malaria Control (DOMC) and national and international partners involved with malaria prevention and control efforts in Kenya. The activities that PMI is proposing to support fit within the DOMC's strategic plan and build on investments made by PMI and other partners to improve and expand malaria-related services. This document briefly reviews the current status of malaria control policies and interventions in Kenya, describes progress to date, identifies challenges and unmet needs that must be addressed to meet the targets of the DOMC and PMI, and provides a description of planned FY 2014 activities.

Malaria Situation in Kenya

Kenya's 2011 population is estimated at 41.6 million people, with an estimated population growth of 2.7% per year.[1] Children under five years of age account for about 16% of the total population.[2] Geographically, the country falls into two main regions: lowland areas, both coastal and around lake basins, and highland areas on both sides of the Great Rift Valley. Kenya has approximately 42 ethnic groups, and is a predominantly agricultural economy with a strong industrial base. Kenya is ranked 145 out of 187 countries on the 2013 United Nation's Human Development Index, which measures life expectancy, adult literacy and per capita income. Life expectancy in Kenya has seen an overall

---

[1] World Bank, http://data.worldbank.org/country/kenya. Public health expenditure consists of recurrent and capital spending from government (central and local) budgets, external borrowings and grants (including donations from international agencies and nongovernmental organizations) and social (or compulsory) health insurance funds.
[2] 2009 Kenya Population and Housing Census Ibid, page 38

downward trend since the late 1980s but has recently increased to 57 years.[1] The HIV/AIDS estimated adult prevalence is 6.2%.[1] The total expenditure on health increased slightly from 4.1% of the gross domestic product in 2004 to 4.5% in 2011.[1] The Government of Kenya's per capita public sector health expenditures in Kenya also rose from $19 in 2000 to $39 in 2011.[1] The mortality rate in children under five years of age has declined by 36% from 115 deaths per 1,000 live births in the 2003 Kenya Demographic and Health Survey (DHS) to 74 deaths per 1,000 observed in the latest 2008–2009 DHS.[3]

Malaria still remains a major public health problem in Kenya. It accounts for about 31% of outpatient consultations and 5% of hospital admissions. Malaria transmission and infection risk in Kenya is determined largely by altitude, rainfall patterns and temperature. Therefore, malaria prevalence varies considerably by season and across geographic regions. The variations in altitude and terrain create contrasts in the country's climate, which ranges from tropical along the coast to temperate in the interior to very dry in the north and northeast. There are two rainy seasons—the long rains occur from April to June and the short rains from October to December. The highest temperatures are from February to March and the lowest from July to August.

All four species of *Plasmodium* infecting humans occur in Kenya. *Plasmodium falciparum*, which causes the most severe form of the disease, is the most common accounting for over 98% of all malaria infections in the country. The major malaria vectors in Kenya are *An. gambiae* complex (*An. gambiae ss, An. arabiensis, An. merus*) and *An. funestus*. The malaria vector distribution in the country is not uniform due to variation in climatic factors, particularly temperature and rainfall.

About 70% of the Kenyan population is at risk for malaria. The majority of the at-risk population (17 million people) lives in areas of epidemic and seasonal malaria transmission where *P. falciparum* parasite prevalence is usually less than 5%. However, an estimated 12 million people live in endemic areas, one-third of whom (~4 million people) live in areas where parasite prevalence is estimated to be equal to or greater than 40%. For the purposes of malaria control, the country has been stratified into four epidemiological zones to address the varied risks:

- **Endemic areas:** These areas of stable malaria have altitudes ranging from 0 to 1,300 meters around Lake Victoria in western Kenya and in the coastal regions of the country. Transmission is intense throughout the year with *P. falciparum* prevalence between 20% to 40% and high annual entomological inoculation rates. Of the total population, 29% lives in a malaria-endemic zone.

- **Highland epidemic-prone areas:** Malaria transmission in the western highlands is seasonal with considerable year-to-year variation. The entire population is vulnerable and case fatality rates during an epidemic can be up to ten times greater than in endemic regions. Approximately 20% of Kenyans live in these areas; the malaria prevalence in these areas ranges from 1% to 5%, but can be as high as 10% to 20%.

---

[3] KNBS and IFC Macro, page 129

- **Seasonal malaria transmission areas:** This epidemiological zone comprises arid and semi-arid areas of northern and southeastern parts of the country which experience short periods of intense malaria transmission during the rainy seasons. Approximately 21% of the population lives within these arid/semi-arid areas of the country; the malaria prevalence is less than 5%.

- **Low malaria risk areas:** This zone covers the central highlands of Kenya including Nairobi. Approximately 30% of the population lives in areas where there is little to no malaria transmission.

The country's 2009 endemicity map (Figure 1, below) depicts the current malaria transmission intensity for the entire country, with high transmission intensity in endemic zones highlighted by the darkly shaded areas. The 2010 Malaria Indicator Survey (MIS) indicated that malaria prevalence in the western lake endemic zone, the darkest area of the map, remained very high at 38%.

Figure 1. 2009 Kenya Malaria Endemicity Map

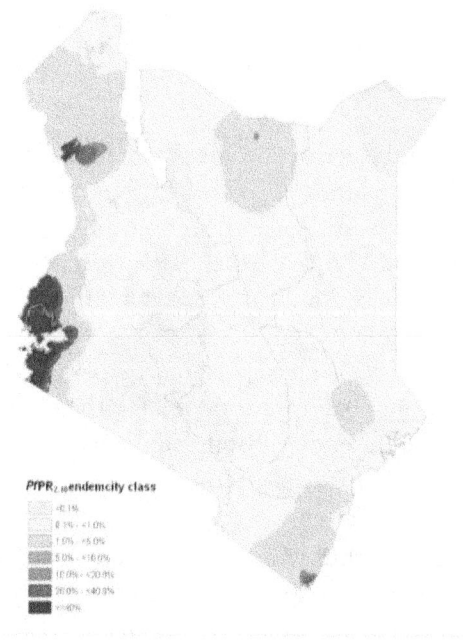

Health System Delivery Structure and Ministry of Health Organization

Service delivery is provided along a continuum of care starting from the household and ending at the country's main referral hospitals through a hierarchy of health care levels, beginning at the dispensary and ending at the national referral hospitals (Figure 2).

Figure 2. Service Delivery Pathway

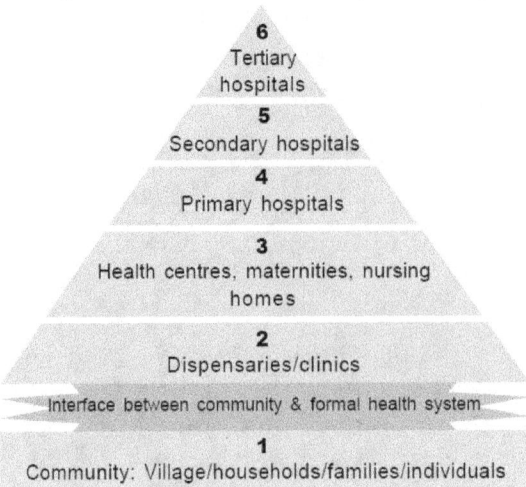

The *Kenya Vision 2030,* the national long-term development plan, guides the country's overall development, including health. Health services in Kenya have been provided through two ministries for the last five years (Ministry of Medical Services and the Ministry of Public Health and Sanitation, following the signing of the National Accord and Reconciliation Act of 2008, and as part of the Government's reorganization process.

Following national and county general elections in March 2013, Kenya began the process of devolution as set forth in the 2010 Constitution of Kenya. The transition to 47 counties from seven provinces as the primary administrative unit has a three-year time line for full implementation guided by a Transitional Authority. At the national level, the current proposal has the Ministry of Public Health and Sanitation and the Ministry of Medical Services merging into one Department of Health with a Cabinet Secretary, Principal Secretary, and Director General. Four directorates are proposed under the Director General. The DOMC is anticipated to be part of the Directorate of Preventive and Promotive Services. Key functions that are proposed for the national level include health policy, national referral health facilities and reference laboratories, disease surveillance, health commodity procurement, capacity building and technical assistance.

The Transitional authority working together with Sectoral Function Assignment and Competency Teams have been trying to establish roles and responsibilities and functions of the national and county governments under devolution. These changes will necessitate the re-alignment of the implementation of PMI interventions to the new administrative units in 2014. The changes will impact on operational costs and human resources shifting roles and responsibilities.

The Division of Malaria Control

The DOMC is currently staffed by technical professionals who are seconded from other departments and divisions in the ministry. The division has six technical units: vector control, diagnosis and case management, malaria in pregnancy, epidemic preparedness and response, advocacy, communication and social mobilization, and surveillance, monitoring and evaluation, and operational research. Each unit has a focal point and one or more technical officers. Although the current structure and staff within the DOMC remains intact, a consolidation of technical units and functions and reassignment of staff to the counties or other programs seems likely to occur.

The Malaria Interagency Coordination Committee is convened biannually by the DOMC on behalf of the Director of Public Health. It includes the other Ministry of Health divisions, non-governmental organizations, community-based organizations, private sector, and development partners. The DOMC also has six primary technical working groups that meet quarterly and are aligned with the six technical units of the division. In addition, the primary technical working groups have the capacity to form sub-committees for more concentrated discussion or work around a particular issue; the sub-committees report back through the primary working group structure. For example, the Advocacy, Communication and Social Mobilization working group started a Resource Mobilization sub-committee in 2013 and the Case Management working group has a standing Diagnostics and Laboratory sub-committee.

County Departments of Health

The proposed structure of a county Department of Health has a Chief Officer for Health overseeing four primary units including Preventive and Promotive Services. The malaria control program and County Malaria Control Coordinator are anticipated to be part of Preventive and Promotive Services. Functions important to malaria control programs that have been transferred to the counties include health services management, communicable and vector-borne disease control and management, and environmental health services. Health financing, health information systems and monitoring and evaluation are expected to be shared functions between the national and county levels. However, the structures and personnel are not yet in place in the counties to implement these functions effectively.

Devolution to county governments will certainly impact the DOMC and PMI beginning in 2013. The administrative changes are likely to impact operational plans and costs as a result of new county-level malaria control programs. The program costs are expected to increase, particularly during the three-year transition phase, as county malaria control programs become functional and DOMC continues to provide support to ensure continuity of operations and implementation of malaria interventions.

Country Malaria Control Strategy

The Government of Kenya (GoK) remains committed to improving health service delivery and places a high priority on malaria control. The GoK has prioritized malaria prevention and treatment interventions and outlined them in the NMS, which has six strategic objectives that together are focused on reaching a two-third reduction of malaria morbidity and mortality by 2017:

- **Objective 1:** By 2013, to have at least 80% of people living in malaria-risk areas using appropriate malaria preventive interventions.

- **Objective 2:** To have 100% of fever cases which present to a health worker receive prompt and effective diagnosis and treatment by 2013.

- **Objective 3:** To ensure that all malaria epidemic-prone districts have the capacity to detect and the ability to respond to malaria epidemics.

- **Objective 4:** To strengthen surveillance, monitoring and evaluation systems so that key malaria indicators are routinely monitored and evaluated in all at-risk malaria districts by 2011.

- **Objective 5:** To strengthen advocacy, communication and social mobilization capacities for malaria control to ensure that at least 80% of people in at-risk areas have knowledge on prevention and treatment of malaria by 2014.

- **Objective 6:** By 2013, to strengthen capacity in program management in order to achieve malaria programmatic objectives at all levels of the health care system.

Strategies to support the achievement of NMS objectives include adopting a multisectoral approach to malaria control; decentralizing malaria control operations to counties beginning in 2013; tailoring interventions to the prevailing epidemiology; and strengthening the malaria control performance monitoring system. Given the varied and changing malaria epidemiology, Kenya is targeting appropriate intervention measures for specific malaria-risk areas. The DOMC has strategically reprioritized the approved malaria control interventions according to malaria risk, in order to target resources towards achieving the highest impact possible.

Kenya Malaria Control Strategy – strategic approach by intervention

Indoor residual spraying

The NMS set a target of 80% of Kenyans at risk of malaria using appropriate malaria prevention interventions, including ITNs and IRS. The NMS has prioritized IRS for malaria-endemic districts with additional support for capacity building and focal IRS in epidemic-prone districts. To ensure that proper IRS activities are carried out, the DOMC and partners identify and train local health personnel who will supervise activities, and spray operators who do the actual spraying. Health workers in epidemic-prone regions will also be trained to use malaria surveillance data to determine priorities for focalized IRS activities. The recent change to a non-pyrethroid insecticide for IRS was based on data indicating widespread, high-level resistance to pyrethroids.

Insecticide-treated nets

The GoK has embraced universal ITN coverage as a strategy to ensure that all groups at risk in malaria-endemic and -epidemic zones have access to long-lasting ITNs through various distribution channels. The target for ITNs is to have at least 80% of people living in malaria-risk areas using appropriate malaria prevention interventions by 2013 through: 1) periodic mass distribution campaigns, carried out every three years to scale up net ownership, where free ITNs are distributed (one net for every two people) to all targeted geographic areas; 2) routine distribution, in which pregnant women and children under one year are given free nets through antenatal care (ANC) clinics and child health clinics; and, 3) social marketing of ITNs, which promotes the sale of subsidized ITNs through social marketing channels, particularly in designated rural areas. Commercial sales of ITNs in the private sector are also endorsed by the DOMC.

Malaria in Pregnancy (MIP)

In 2009, the GoK changed the national policy to ensure that MIP interventions are implemented in endemic areas. The 2010 MIS results showed improved, though continued low, coverage of IPTp; only 25% of pregnant women receive two or more doses of sulfadoxine-pyrimethamine (SP), despite high ANC attendance (86% of women attend ANC two or more times during their pregnancy). The 2010 National Guidelines for the Diagnosis, Treatment and Prevention of Malaria in Kenya emphasize the integration of MIP in the overall ANC package for maternal health that includes IPTp, ITNs, prompt diagnosis and treatment of fever due to malaria, and behavior change communication. There has been renewed attention to MIP with the World Health Organization (WHO) guidelines released in 2012. The Division of Malaria Control will review the national guidelines and update these in line with the new WHO guidance.

Case Management

The 2010 National Guidelines for the Diagnosis, Treatment and Prevention of Malaria in Kenya recommend diagnosis-based treatment as part of effective case management. The NMS target for case management is to ensure that 100% of all fever cases receive a parasitological diagnosis, by microscopy or rapid diagnostic test (RDT), and effective treatment by 2013. To support this objective, Kenya implemented a national rollout of RDTs to health dispensaries and health centers in late 2012, provides first-line ACTs for all public health facilities, and supports national in-service training for diagnostics and case management. The NMS target for community case management is to have at least 80% of self-managed fever cases (i.e., persons with fever who seek care outside of the traditional health care system from pharmacies or informal drug outlets) receive prompt and effective treatment by 2013. To support this objective, the DOMC is working with the GoK and partners to make RDTs and ACTs available to community health workers to discourage use of informal drug outlets by persons with fever and in the private sector through subsidy schemes to encourage diagnosis prior to treatment. To improve home management of malaria, the NMS proposed that community health workers (CHWs) receive training and supportive supervision for malaria case management, prevention, BCC, record keeping and reporting. First-line malaria treatment and RDTs will be integrated into the CHW kit, and all CHWs will be linked to the nearest health facility for resupply of commodities, supervision, monitoring and referral.

Monitoring and Evaluation, and Operational Research

Monitoring and evaluation and operational research are vital assessment elements for tracking the progress of malaria control activities. The DOMC has developed a comprehensive M&E Plan to accompany the NMS, which recommends the frequency and methodology of monitoring key program indicators for each of the interventions in order to better assess and inform program implementation. Operational research is carried out to provide more information and answer questions where appraisals are needed to determine the most appropriate approaches for interventions. Operational research has included the following: social behavior in malaria control; entomological studies; tracking changes in malaria transmission; piloting school-based malaria parasite control; insecticide resistance; malaria early warning systems; and cost-effectiveness analysis of different combinations of control interventions.

With the Health Information System's DHIS2 platform up and running, the DOMC and all major partner efforts at surveillance and routine health facility data collection will be based on this system in order to consolidate data collection and improve reporting efforts.

<u>Behavior Change and Communication</u>

Behavior change and communication is a cross-cutting activity that plays a role in each of the malaria control interventions. These activities ensure that beneficiaries have correct and timely information about the use and importance of each intervention offered as part of malaria control. Implementation of BCC activities will focus on the involvement health providers and community health workers in malaria control and preventive activities, more emphasis will be placed on using interpersonal communication approaches in order to get personal insights on the use of malaria control interventions. In addition, other channels of communication (e.g., television, radio, print, mobile phones) will be used. The national target is to strengthen advocacy, communication and social mobilization capacities for malaria control to ensure that at least 80% of people in malarious areas have knowledge on prevention and treatment of malaria by 2013.

Integration, Collaboration and Coordination

The US Government team in Kenya has developed a strategy that embraces a whole-of-government, multi-layer communication strategy, reflecting all fundamental principles of PMI. The Peace Corps, Department of Defense, Department of Health and Human Services/Centers for Disease Control (CDC), Department of State, US Agency for International Development (USAID) and President's Emergency Plan for AIDS Relief (PEPFAR) have implemented and reported on a large program base for several years. This tight, multi-tiered governance structure allows for full participation across agencies, at all levels, and across technical areas – resulting in programs that are responsive to country needs. Examples include:

- PMI/Kenya and the DOMC have worked closely with the Walter Reed Army Institute of Research to support and strengthen Kenya's malaria diagnostic capacity for both RDTs and microscopy. PMI-supported activities have included: the procurement and distribution of microscopes, malaria microscopy training, quality assurance raining, development and production of the National Guidelines on Parasitological Diagnosis of Malaria and Malaria Vector Surveillance in Kenya (2013) and accompanying microscopy wall charts and job aids, and implementation of the quality assurance program for malaria diagnostics through supportive supervision and on-the-job training.

- PMI/Kenya has partnered with Peace Corps since 2011 to support joint malaria activities. PMI supported three Peace Corps-recruited malaria volunteers in 2012 who worked closely with the DOMC, district malaria control coordinators, community health extension workers (CHEWs) who supervise community health workers, CHWs, and other stakeholders to support community-based malaria control activities. Coordinated by the three PMI-supported malaria volunteers, more than 70 Peace Corps volunteers across Kenya hosted 2013 World Malaria Day activities with over 10,000 participants from local communities.

In addition to US Government integration and collaboration, PMI/Kenya facilitates coordination of activities among partners in malaria control in Kenya, including: Global Fund, research institutions, non-governmental organizations, World Health Organization (WHO), the United Kingdom's Department for International Development (DFID), private sector and other development partners. PMI is an integral partner to the DOMC and actively participates in annual planning and reviews, technical working groups, interagency coordination committees, and other stakeholder related activities.

Financial support for the DOMC's plan will come from three primary sources: Global Fund, DFID and PMI. While funding for Phase 2 of the Global Fund Round 10 grant will not be finalized until mid-2014, it is estimated that the annual grant funding level will be about $30 million. DFID has pledged a total of $40 million over three years to support the GoK's IRS program. Based on the budget analysis and the contributions from Global Fund and DFID, PMI/Kenya has concluded that its FY 2014 budget ($32.4 million) will be required to fill critical program gaps. The available funding (totaling about $80 million) that will support the DOMC's annual malaria control plan falls short of the expected need, which for this coming year is estimated to be $297 million. As discussed throughout this operational plan, the PMI FY 2014 funded activities have been prioritized after considering the funding available from other donor programs to ensure the most critical activities are funded.

PMI Goals, Targets and Indicators

The goal of PMI is to reduce malaria-associated mortality by 70% compared to pre-Initiative levels in the 15 original PMI countries, including Kenya, and to reduce malaria-associated mortality by 50% in countries added to PMI in FY 2010 and later. By the end of 2014, PMI will have assisted Kenya in making progress to achieve the following targets in populations at risk for malaria:

- >90% of households with a pregnant woman and/or children under five will own at least one ITN;
- 85% of children under five will have slept under an ITN the previous night;
- 85% of pregnant women will have slept under an ITN the previous night;
- 85% of houses in geographic areas targeted for IRS will have been sprayed;
- 85% of pregnant women and children under five will have slept under an ITN the previous night or in a house that has been sprayed with IRS in the last 12 months;
- 85% of women who have completed a pregnancy in the last two years will have received two or more doses of IPTp during that pregnancy;
- 85% of government health facilities will have ACTs available for treatment of uncomplicated malaria; and
- 85% of children under five with suspected or confirmed malaria will have received treatment with ACTs within 24 hours of onset of their symptoms.

Progress on Coverage/Impact Indicators to Date

In Kenya, coverage with effective interventions and the health impact are measured largely through national household surveys. The 2008–2009 DHS and 2010 MIS provided evidence of Kenya's progress in achieving national targets (Table 1).

Table 1. Summary of Selected Malaria Indicators

	2003 DHS[a]	2007 MIS[b]	2008–09 DHS[c]	2010 MIS
Proportion of households with at least one ITN	6%	48%	56%	48%
Proportion of children under five years old who slept under an ITN the previous night	5%	39%	47%	42%
Proportion of pregnant women who slept under an ITN the previous night	4%	40%	49%	41%
Proportion of women who received two or more doses of sulfadoxine-pyrimethamine (SP) during their last pregnancy in the last two years at least one of which was received during an ANC visit	4%	13%	14%	25%
Proportion of children under five years old with fever in the last two weeks who received treatment with ACTs within 24 hours of onset of fever	N/A	4%	4%	11%
All-cause under-five mortality	115 per 1000 live births	--	74 per 1000 live births	--

[a] Pre-PMI baseline data for all-cause under-five mortality
[b] PMI baseline data for coverage indicators
[c] PMI baseline data for all-cause under-five mortality

Other Relevant Evidence of Progress

At the request of the DOMC, PMI supported a reanalysis of the 1998, 2003 and 2008–09 DHS survey data to assess determinants of childhood mortality in Kenya between 1998 and 2008. This analysis, completed in December 2012, found that infant and under-five mortality in Kenya was largely unchanged between 1998 and 2003 but declined significantly between 2003 and 2008. The main determinants that contributed to a decline in infant and under-five mortality were an increase in the use of mosquito nets among children under five, an increase in levels of full immunization of children, and an increase in the use of contraception among mothers. A white paper published by the World Bank in May 2012, also found ITN ownership contributed to mortality declines in Kenya between 2003 and 2008, concluding that the increased ownership of ITNs in malaria-endemic zones explains 39% of the decline in post-neonatal mortality and 58% of the decline in infant mortality[4].

Challenges, Opportunities and Threats

Challenges

Within the devolution context, one of the challenges will be to ensure that the county governments continue to prioritize malaria control interventions and invest resources in prevention and treatment. This will be particularly critical in endemic and epidemic-prone counties. The key malaria partners in Kenya, including PMI, recently supported the development of county malaria profiles that will be used to advocate with county governments. Working with counties to prioritize and fund malaria

---

[4] What has driven the infant mortality decline in Kenya? G. Demombynes and S.K. Trommlerová. *The World Bank. Policy Research Working Paper 6057.* May 2012.

control activities will be essential to safeguard the gains made nationally in malaria control during this transition period.

Strengthening malaria diagnosis, treatment and reporting remains a challenge. Recent PMI support to strengthening data collection and reporting on the use of ACTs and RDTs through the District Health Information System (DHIS2) system increased the reporting from health facilities from ~40% to 70%. Although RDTs were rolled out nationally in late 2012, not all health facilities had received them by April 2013. Progress toward national RDT implementation stalled when over half of the RDT supply for 2013 was lost in a central warehouse fire. The loss of those RDTs was a setback for the program and will likely result in stock outs and delayed integration of RDTs into the malaria community case management strategy.

Opportunities

Although devolution to county government structures might lead to uncertainties and disruptions in the short term, county government offers an opportunity to deliver health services directly to constituents and communities in a transparent and accountable manner. One of the basic tenets of devolution is to ensure resources and services are appropriately used and delivered in the communities. The malaria control program could potentially benefit from devolution. For example, counties could harness additional resources outside of the health system such as teachers and schools to deliver commodities (e.g., ITNs) or for high-profile labor-intense strategies such as IRS. As county governments evolve, advocacy and support for malaria activities by partners and donors also will be critical. The PMI/Kenya team anticipates that additional resources will be required to initiate county malaria control programs over the transition period with the longer-term objective that counties will earmark resources to sustain and scale up malaria control interventions.

Over the last decade, there has been substantial political commitment at the national level for malaria control. It is expected that this support will continue and that the Department of Health will continue to prioritize malaria as one of the key health interventions. With a limited number of health functions remaining at the national level, PMI/Kenya and partners have an opportunity to focus on strengthening critical areas such as policy, surveillance and monitoring and evaluation. It will be imperative to ensure that planned activities are implemented and conditions set by the Global Fund and other partners are met to avoid disruptions in funding and negative impact on the national malaria control program.

Threats

An estimated 35% of the Kenya health budget is donor supported[5] and most of the key malaria interventions are currently supported by donors. This presents a threat in a context of declining global donations and financing. It is critical that the national and county governments earmark resources to invest in malaria prevention and control activities to ensure sustainability.

In 2012, Kenya changed their national policy on IRS due to increasing insecticide resistance to pyerethroids. The new policy dictates a more expensive insecticide and twice a year spraying cycles, which substantially increases operational costs. As a result, PMI will have to scale down the geographical areas that had previously been sprayed despite an increase in total IRS resources due to pooled contributions from DFID and PMI. The increased insecticide and operational costs will

---

[5] Kenya National Health Accounts 2009/2010, Ministry of Health.

reduce the scope of IRS activities and limit the potential value of this intervention. Kenya is in the process of developing a National Strategic Plan on Insecticide Resistance; the costs associated with non-pyrethroid insecticides will continue to be a threat to implementation of large-scale IRS activities in the country.

PMI Support Strategy

PMI supports all key malaria interventions in Kenya and has been one of the key partners over the last six years. PMI/Kenya strategically focuses on integration, partnership and flexibility. A large proportion of PMI-supported activities are implemented through projects that also include other health domains (e.g., health system strengthening, community health, and health communications and promotion). This helps promote a rational use of US Government resources, avoids having multiple vertical programs, and fosters synergy with other Ministry of Health entities.

Since the beginning of the program in Kenya, PMI has procured ACTs, RDTs and ITNs for targeted health facilities and provided the commodities cost-free to end-users, in line with the national strategy. PMI support in these areas has been critical in addressing gaps based on the funding of the other key partner, Global Fund. PMI support has averted stock outs and in some cases, led to the scale up of critical interventions such as the mass campaign distribution of ITNs in 2011.

PMI support will continue to strengthen other interventions such as social mobilization, BCC, MIP, and monitoring and evaluation. PMI will also support health systems strengthening at national and county levels, especially to improve reporting on malaria commodities.

OPERATIONAL PLAN

Indoor Residual Spraying

DOMC/PMI Objectives

The NMS set a target of 80% of Kenyans living at risk of malaria using appropriate malaria prevention interventions, including ITNs and IRS. The NMS has prioritized IRS for malaria-endemic districts with additional support for capacity building and focal IRS in epidemic-prone districts.

Progress since PMI was launched

The PMI IRS program in Kenya began in 2008. PMI supported IRS in focal areas in 16 highland districts. PMI assumed responsibility for blanket spraying of two highland districts and one lowland endemic district, which bordered the highlands, as an initial phase to create a buffer between the lowland endemic districts and the highland epidemic districts where IRS was planned to be phased out. PMI sprayed the same three districts in 2009.

In 2010, the DOMC assumed responsibility for IRS in the highlands, and PMI supported IRS in three lowland districts including the lowland district that had been previously sprayed by PMI in 2008 and 2009. The same three lowland districts were sprayed in 2011 and 2012. A fourth lowland district was sprayed for the first time in 2012. All PMI-supported IRS consisted of blanket spraying of the target areas. The target populations and annual spray coverage percentages are provided in Table 2.

Table 2. Indoor Residual Spray Program Coverage Areas Targeted By the President's Malaria Initiative, 2008–2012

Year	Targeted Areas	Targeted Households	Targeted Population	Coverage
2008	2 highland districts, 1 lowland district	764,050	3,061,967[1]	96%
2009	2 highland districts, 1 lowland district	517,051	1,435,272	94.6%
2010	3 lowland districts	503,707	1,892,725	97.1%
2011	3 lowland districts	485,043	1,832,090	89%
2012	4 lowland districts	692,258	2,189,275	98%

1. The 2008 targeted population includes those covered by the Government of Kenya's IRS program, which received PMI support. The GoK program ended after the 2008 spray round, leaving PMI as supporting the only IRS program in Kenya.

From 2008 to 2012, the IRS program used pyrethroid insecticides. Pyrethroid resistance had been detected in *An. gambiae* s.s. in western Kenya but this species was significantly reduced by ITNs and was largely absent in the districts targeted for IRS. This species was most common in areas near the Ugandan border. By late 2012, however, PMI supported entomological monitoring showed that the range of *An. gambiae* s.s. was expanding eastward. Furthermore, pyrethroid resistance was observed in *An. funestus* as well as in *An. arabiensis* in one district that had been sprayed for four consecutive years. Given the increasing pyrethroid resistance in western Kenya, the DOMC decided to shift from one annual round of IRS with pyrethroids to two annual rounds with a non-pyrethroid insecticide beginning in 2013.

Progress in the last 12 months

In 2012, IRS operations were targeted to four districts in the lowland, lake endemic region of western Kenya. A total of 693,060 structures were sprayed representing 98% of identified structures. A total of 2,435,836 people resided in areas protected by the IRS program in 2012.

In 2013, IRS was delayed because of logistical issues concerning the change of insecticide. The next round will be conducted in February and March of 2014, just before the long rains. With co-funding from DFID, two counties will be targeted in 2013-2014. DFID resources will be used to spray Homa Bay County and PMI resources will be used to spray the selected sub-counties in Migori County. These two counties include three of the four districts that were sprayed in 2012. It is estimated that 555,473 structures will be sprayed and 1,995,149 people will be reached in each of the two rounds of IRS.

Entomological monitoring was conducted in 16 sites in western Kenya including 14 sites within the IRS districts. Pyrethroid resistance was confirmed in *An. gambiae* s.s and increasing pyrethroid resistance was also observed in *An. arabiensis*. Furthermore, *An. funestus* has become increasingly common and pyrethroid resistance has been observed in this species as well. Data on insecticide resistance are provided in Table 3, below.

Challenges, Opportunities and Threats

The change to a non-pyrethroid insecticide was necessary because of the emergence of pyrethroid resistance throughout much of western Kenya. The selection of a non-pyrethroid insecticide for IRS will increase the cost of the program as the insecticide itself is more expensive than pyrethroids, and the shorter duration may require up to two rounds of spraying per year rather than one. However, DFID has committed funds to augment the PMI-funded IRS operations in Kenya through 2016. With co-funding from DFID, the 2013-2014 IRS operations will reach approximately 83% of the population targeted in 2012. Nyando District, which is now part of Kisumu County, will not be sprayed in 2013-2014.

The shift in governance from a malaria control program managed at the national level to one managed at the county level presents an additional challenge as the counties will need to develop a unified approach to IRS and, in particular, insecticide resistance management strategies. However, the DOMC will develop national policy that will help guide counties in implementation of IRS. Because IRS operations will be managed at the county level, there are opportunities to train local staff on the management and implementation of IRS and may allow for the eventual transfer of IRS operations to county governments.

Table 3. Summary of WHO susceptibility assays on *Anopheles gambiae s.l.* against three classes of insecticide in counties in western Kenya, 2012

County	Sublocation	Insecticide	Number Tested	24-Hour Mortality	Resistance Status[a]
Kisumu[b]	Nyando	Deltamethrin	98	71	Resistant
		Permethrin	99	41	Resistant
		Bendiocarb	100	100	Susceptible
		Malathion	100	100	Susceptible
	Muhoroni	Deltamethrin	100	78	Resistant
		Permethrin	100	80	Resistant
	Nyakach	Permethrin	99	89	Resistant
Homa Bay[b]	Marindi	Deltamethrin	168	74	Resistant
		Permethrin	46	52	Resistant
	Ndhiwa	Deltamethrin	116	39	Resistant
		Permethrin	89	75	Resistant
	Rachuonyo	Deltamethrin	538	80	Resistant
		Permethrin	122	85	Resistant
		Malathion	60	98	Susceptible
Migori[b]	Nyatike	Bendiocarb	35	100	Susceptible
		Deltamethrin	187	73	Resistant
		Permethrin	97	64	Resistant
	Rongo	Deltamethrin	53	60	Resistant
		Permethrin	49	71	Resistant
Bungoma	Bungoma	Deltamethrin	100	67	Resistant
Busia	Teso North	Deltamethrin	147	66	Resistant
		Permethrin	62	87	Resistant
	Teso South	Deltamethrin	191	78	Resistant
		Permethrin	58	75	Resistant
Siaya	Bondo	Deltamethrin	416	50	Resistant
		Permethrin	91	77	Resistant
	Rarieda	Deltamethrin	267	90	Suspected resistant
		Permethrin	103	56	Resistant

[a] Resistance status is based on the updated guidelines recommended in the WHO document "Test procedures for insecticide resistance monitoring in malaria vector mosquitoes": greater than 98% mortality in tube bioassays indicates full susceptibility, 90-97% mortality indicates probable resistance, and less than 90% mortality indicates resistance to the insecticide being tested.

[b] Indicates counties that were sprayed or partially sprayed in 2012 (west Kisumu County was not sprayed in 2012).

Proposed PMI Activities with FY 2014 Funding: ($8,336,000)

With FY 2014 funding and co-funding from DfID, PMI will spray up to three endemic counties. PMI will also provide support to continue entomological monitoring in the targeted county. Specific activities include:

1. **IRS implementation and management:** Support up to two rounds of IRS with a non-pyrethroid insecticide in up to three endemic counties with a target of 85% coverage in targeted areas. The IRS program will be co-funded and coordinated with DFID. Based on the cost of the insecticide and two rounds of spraying annually, the estimated population coverage will be almost two million people living in 555,000 households. *($7,980,200)*

2. **Entomological monitoring of IRS effectiveness in sprayed sub-county areas:** Given the expansion of IRS in lowland areas of western Kenya, the detection of insecticide resistance in several areas of western Kenya and the recent switch toIRS with non-pyrethroid insecticides, PMI will continue entomologic and insecticide resistance monitoring in 14 sites in western Kenya. Monitoring will include determination of species and abundance, insecticide resistance testing and duration of efficacy of insecticides sprayed on walls. *($330,000)*

3. **Technical assistance—CDC:** Support two visits from CDC to provide technical assistance to the entomological monitoring program and specifically, IRS implementation activities. *($24,000)*

Insecticide-Treated Nets

DOMC/PMI Objectives

The NMS stated objective is to attain universal coverage of ITNs, defined as reaching a ratio of one ITN for every two people, in conjunction with increasing use of those nets to 80%, within prioritized counties by 2013. Universal coverage is to be achieved through multiple distribution channels, including:

- Periodic free mass distribution of ITNs: In 2011-2012, a rolling universal coverage mass distribution campaign was conducted in three different phases distributed over 11 million ITNs to targeted areas. A replacement mass distribution campaign is scheduled to be conducted in 2014, but given funding delays may be moved to 2015.

- Routine distribution to vulnerable populations: Routine distribution is targeted for all vulnerable populations living in malaria-endemic and epidemic-prone areas in Kenya, and exceeds the geographic areas targeted in the mass distribution campaign. Currently, the DOMC supports routine distribution of free ITNs to pregnant women and children through an estimated 3,500 targeted ANC and child health clinics. ITNs are also distributed to persons living with HIV/AIDS as part of the standard package of care provided through comprehensive care clinics. Routine distribution remains the primary channel for access to free ITNs between mass distribution campaigns. However, the number of households reached through these routine channels is not sufficient to maintain universal coverage. Consequently, Kenya is developing a community-based continuous distribution channel to replace nets in targeted households in a cost-effective manner to help maintain high coverage levels, with an ultimate goal of reducing the need for mass distribution campaigns.

- Social marketing of ITNs: Through a private sector partner, DFID has supported a small social marketing program, which sells about 600,000 ITNs per year through community-based organizations in targeted areas. These ITNs sell for KSh 50 ($0.70) each and are primarily sold in rural areas in endemic and epidemic-prone counties. The DOMC estimates that demand for socially-marketed nets exceeds current supply levels and that this program could be expanded.

- Commercial sales: ITNs can be found in the commercial market in urban supermarkets and retail outlets where they are sold at full price. The DOMC supports strategies to promote a sustainable ITN market, including decreased taxes and tariffs on netting material and development and airing of generic demand-creation messages from which manufacturers can promote their individual brands.

ITN Coverage and Use

Data from MIS and DHS surveys over the past decade have shown considerable progress in access to ITNs. Insecticide-treated net ownership increased from 6% in 2003 to 48% in the 2010 MIS. Likewise, the ITN use among pregnant women (41%) and children under five years of age (42%) has also remained stable from the 2007 MIS, when use was ~40% for both target groups. Following the 2011 mass distribution campaign, a household survey found that the campaign increased household ownership in rural areas from an average of one ITN per household to 2.6 ITNs per household. The survey estimated that universal coverage had been achieved in 67% of households in the targeted campaign areas and confirmed that the campaign ensured equitable net distribution across all wealth quintiles. It is expected that the impact of the 2011 mass distribution campaign will be documented in the 2013 DHS.

Although the campaign was successful in dramatically increasing household ownership of ITNs, the post-campaign household survey, which was conducted in the dry season, documented surprisingly low ITN use; overall the proportion of children under five years of age who slept under an ITN the night before the survey was just 26%. A follow-up qualitative study (dissemination pending) has found that inconsistent net use was driven by three primary factors: a low risk perception in the dry season, the absence of caregivers at night to put the children under the net, and disruption of sleeping patterns caused by visitors. The DOMC will use the results of the household survey and qualitative study to develop appropriate communication messages and programs to encourage correct and consistent use of ITNs every night.

Progress in the last 12 months

Continuous Distribution: PMI continues to support the DOMC's routine distribution program, to ensure that vulnerable populations (i.e. pregnant women and children under one) have consistent access to ITNs. In the past 12 months, PMI has procured 1.72 million ITNs for distribution through the routine system, building upon previous investments. An estimated 1.3 million of these ITNs will be distributed by September 2013. The balance of ITNs will be distributed in early 2014.

PMI continues to partner with DFID to ensure that 100% of the ITN needs for distribution through the routine system are fully met. The DOMC is developing alternative ITN distribution channels that will allow households to request replacement nets from the public health system on an as-needed basis (see further details below under proposed FY 2014 funded activities).

ITN Use: Based on the very low ITN use documented in the 2011 post-campaign survey, PMI supported a qualitative study to understand the reasons behind the low ITN use findings. As discussed in greater detail in the BCC section (below), over the past year PMI continued to support focused, intensive interpersonal communication efforts in the highest-priority areas to improve the consistent use of ITNs among all family members. Specific communication campaigns are being designed to address the consistent use issue and will be implemented in the coming year.

Challenges, Opportunities and Threats

The planned 2014-2015 replacement mass distribution campaign should ensure that Kenya will benefit from sustained high ITN coverage in targeted endemic counties. This level of ITN coverage offers opportunities for Kenya to decrease the incidence of malaria in the most highly affected areas. However, the sustained coverage is threatened as the funding for ITN programs in 2015 remains largely undefined. The disbursement of Phase 2 funds from the Global Fund Grant is delayed until mid-2014, which will have a significant impact on the timing of the campaign and likely push the start date back to the end of the calendar year. As of writing, only about 50% of the funds needed to implement the next mass distribution campaign has been identified, which may require the campaign to be rolled out in phases. Another key operational challenge for Kenya will be to develop a systematic way of replacing worn-out nets among targeted households. Establishing a comprehensive continuous distribution system to replace nets in targeted households in a cost effective manner is a critical step in maintaining high coverage levels and removing the need for mass distribution campaigns over the long run. Devolution and the future management of ITNs at the county level will greatly impact the implementation of this intervention—both in the mass distribution campaign as well as in routine/continuous distribution channels. PMI will remain attentive to this issue.

Commodity Gap Analysis

As detailed in Table 4, the ITN gap analysis for FY 2014 highlights the mass campaign replacement needs for at-risk populations living in targeted malaria counties. Assuming that the mass distribution is postponed to 2015, PMI estimates that there will be a 7.8 million ITN gap, based on the estimated population growth and the national policy to fully replace nets 36 months after distribution. For the routine distribution system, an estimated 50% of the annual need remains unmet. DFID's routine net program will end in March 2015, and DFID has not yet made an ITN funding commitment beyond 2014. This is expected to be clarified in 2014. PMI will use its FY 2014 ITNs to meet the distribution needs in a rational manner, recognizing that significant ITN gaps will remain.

Table 4. FY 2014 Insecticide Treated Net Gap Analysis Table

Data Inputs	Country data
A. Targeted 2014-15 Mass Distribution Campaign (Targeted Counties Only)	
Population at risk in 2014	21,399,876
Total number of ITNs needed	12,221,707
Viable ITNs from previous years (assumes all 2011—2012 campaign nets will be expired and need to be replaced)	0
Total estimated available ITNs in-country	
Global Fund, Round 10, Phase 2	4,409,000
PMI FY 2013	500,000
PMI FY 2014	500,000
Mass distribution campaign ITN gap	6,812,707
B. ANC/Child Health Clinic Routine Distribution (for pregnant women and children under one living in targeted areas)	
Population at risk in 2015 (Routine System)	2,901,581
Total number of ITNs needed (Routine System)	2,901,581
Viable ITNs from previous years	0
Pledged ITNs for 2015 distribution	
PMI FY 2014	1,300,000
Routine distribution ITN gap	**1,601,581**
Data Source: 2010 Global Fund Round 10 Kenya Proposal, and DOMC	

Plans and justification

With FY 2014 funds, PMI and DOMC will focus efforts on maintaining a continuous supply of nets and a robust routine distribution system for ITNs as described above, while contributing to the 2014-2015 mass campaign. PMI will also support communications activities to inform the population about how to acquire nets and to promote correct and consistent use. These activities are described further in the Behavior Change Communication section.

Proposed PMI Activities with FY 2014 Funding: ($8,650,000)
1. **Procure ITNs for continuous distribution and the 2014-2015 mass distribution campaign:** Fill 45% of the ITN gap for routine distribution and a portion of the mass campaign gap by purchasing 1.8 million ITNs. These ITNs will be distributed free-of-charge to households located in the geographic area covered by the mass campaign, and to pregnant women and children under one year of age through ANC and child health clinics (routine program). ($6,550,000)

2. **Logistic and program support for ITN distribution to the routine and mass campaign activities**: Provide logistic support, including transportation and storage of nets, for distribution of the 1.8 million ITNs both within the national routine distribution system and for the 2014-2015 mass campaign. ($1,800,000)

3. **Support continuous distribution systems**: Following the completion of the pilot activity in 2014 (per activities supported in the FY 2012 and FY 2013 Malaria Operational Plans), support the adoption of a nationally-approved, community-based continuous distribution channel within all targeted counties. The vision of this new community-based distribution channel will be to have families approach a trained CHW when a net needs to be replaced. The CHW will confirm that an ITN needs to be replaced and provide a voucher to the household member. The household will then redeem the voucher at the health facility for a new net provided free of charge. The design work and plans for this activity are currently underway and expected to begin by the end of 2013. The FY 2014 funding will be used to establish national guidelines and policy, and support for adoption of this program in all targeted counties, which will include training-of-trainers and the publication of job aids. The goal will be to facilitate adoption of this program so that populations living in targeted counties will be able to replace ITNs as they wear out, with the ultimate goal of ending the need for mass campaigns to keep ITN coverage at optimal levels. ($300,000)

4. **Behavior change for correct and consistent use of ITNs**: Support and expand targeted community BCC and social mobilization to increase demand for and uptake of ITNs. Messages and mode of dissemination will be dependent on the venue and target group. Interpersonal communication will be used in health facilities and ANC clinics for patients, in homes during visits by community health workers, and at *barazas* (i.e. community meetings) in villages and during public gatherings where messages are delivered through public address systems. Promoting correct and consistent use of ITNs will be a primary focus of this effort. (This activity is budgeted under the BCC section)

Malaria in Pregnancy (MIP)

DOMC/PMI Objectives

Kenya's MIP program is based on a close working relationship between the Division of Reproductive Health and the DOMC. In the new devolved context, the role of the two divisions will be to set policies and strategies and to ensure that implementation of activities is monitored both at county and national levels. Prevention of MIP is an integral component of the focused ANC approach in Kenya. The 2008-2009 DHS showed that 92% of women in Kenya receive ANC from a medical professional during pregnancy; however, only 15% of women obtain care in the first trimester. Overall, only 47% of pregnant women make four or more ANC visits during pregnancy, with the median gestational age at first visit being 5.7 months.

The NMS has a 2014 target of 80% of people living in malaria-risk areas using appropriate malaria prevention interventions. However, the uptake of IPTp in Kenya has remained low. The results from the most recent 2008-2009 DHS indicate that approximately 34% of women who had a live birth in the preceding two years received any SP dose during an ANC visit. The proportion of pregnant women receiving the recommended two or more doses of SP for IPTp increased from 14% in 2008-2009 (DHS) to 25% in 2010 (MIS). While ANC visits provide an opportunity for administration of IPTp doses, additional community-based MIP activities began with PMI support in 2011. These activities include MIP messaging, use of community data collection tools to capture IPTp uptake, and referral of pregnant women to health facilities to access IPTp services.

The first-line treatment for malaria in pregnancy is oral quinine in the first trimester of pregnancy and artemether-lumefantrine (AL) or oral quinine in the second and third trimesters. The DOMC recommends that pregnant women receive diagnosis by blood smear for malaria, ferrous sulfate (200mcg) and folic acid (5mg) at their second and third ANC visits, and evaluation for anemia during their first and fourth ANC visits.

The recent World Health Organization (WHO) updated policy on IPTp in 2012 recommends IPTp with SP in areas of moderate-to-high malaria transmission for all pregnant women at each scheduled antenatal care visit. WHO recommends a schedule of four antenatal care visits and the first IPTp-SP dose should be administered as early as possible during the second trimester of gestation. In addition each SP dose should be given at least one month apart and that the last dose of IPTp with SP can be administered up to the time of delivery, without safety concerns. Though the revised 2010 National Guidelines for the Diagnosis, Treatment and Prevention of Malaria in Kenya emphasize the integration of MIP in the overall ANC package for maternal health that includes IPTp, ITNs, prompt diagnosis and treatment of fever due to malaria, and health education, the DOMC plans to review the guidelines in line with the updated WHO policy.

Progress in the last 12 months
With the support of PMI, 1,135 health care workers, 32 facility-based service providers, 45 CHEWs and 1,058 CHWs, have been oriented and trained on prevention of malaria in pregnancy in 12 sub-counties (i.e. former districts) in Homa Bay and Bungoma Counties. At the national level, 27 trainers have been educated on malaria in pregnancy. This cadre of trained personnel will be critical in the scale up of MIP interventions at the county level. PMI has also strengthened collection and analysis of MIP data at health-facility and community levels. MIP BCC materials have also been disseminated in the three malaria-endemic regions (i.e. Coast, Nyanza and Western).

Challenges, Opportunities and Threats
The change in MIP policy in 2009 to focus the provision of IPTp to pregnant women in malaria-endemic areas offered an opportunity for the country to focus and scale up these efforts. The simplified guidelines developed by PMI-supported implementing partners are an important base on which to scale up IPTp delivery in all endemic areas. The roll out of the community health strategy offers an opportunity to improve early ANC attendance and access to IPTp. Given the low cost of SP, the GoK has procured SP and no stock outs have been experienced over the last three years. The primary challenges are scaling up IPTp interventions in all endemic areas to reach the 80% target and monitoring and tracking IPTp doses and coverage accurately.

Plans and justification
PMI supports the implementation of MIP interventions, strengthening of ANC healthcare worker capacity in endemic areas, dissemination of simplified guidelines that accompany a "memo" on IPTp, providing guidance to health workers from the Ministry of Health, and supportive supervision. In addition, PMI supports Kenya's community strategy whereby CHEWs and CHWs are trained on the MIP package to mobilize, refer, track and report on pregnant women and ANC attendance in their communities. The combined approach of using CHWs, CHEWs and healthcare

worker orientations through the "memo" and simplified guidelines and supportive supervision helps ensure that pregnant women attend ANC and receive IPTp and ITNs, in addition to other health services as necessary.

In the context of devolved government, health service delivery activities will be implemented at the county level. While PMI will continue to support MIP at the national level, FY 2014 funding is also expected to ensure the scale up of IPTp delivery in two target counties: Homa Bay and Bungoma. The expectation of PMI is that the county governments will then be responsible for these activities and in subsequent years activities will be undertaken in other counties.

Proposed activities with FY 2014 funding: ($700,000)

1. **Sensitize and train healthcare workers on MIP simplified guidelines and IPTp "memo":** All healthcare workers and CHEWs in Homa Bay and Bugoma counties will be sensitized and oriented on MIP using the memo and simplified guidelines. An estimated total of 2,500 healthcare workers will be reached. The orientation will include the use of the Ministry of Health IPTp memo and the current simplified MIP guidelines that have been developed and produced with PMI support. *($250,000)*

2. **Sensitize, orientate, and supervise CHWs:** This activity will include the orientation and training of CHWs on Community Malaria in Pregnancy. CHWs are trained to undertake BCC activities and to refer and track pregnant women to ensure that they receive IPTp at health facilities. An estimated 4,000 CHWs will be sensitized and oriented using the community strategy and other innovative community approaches. The target is to reach approximately 40,000 women of reproductive age with community MIP messages and services. *($400,000)*

3. **Strengthen national and county level policy and monitoring capacity:** Though most of the activity implementation will be at county level, limited support will be provided at the national level in the areas of policy and monitoring of MIP-specific activities. It is also expected that technical support will be provided to counties on MIP, as necessary. *($50,000)*

Case Management

DIAGNOSIS

DOMC/PMI Objectives

In line with Kenya's NMS of ensuring that all patients with fever and suspected malaria receive a diagnostic test before treatment is prescribed, PMI has supported the procurement and distribution of RDTs to health dispensaries and health centers (i.e., Levels 2 and 3) and implementation of quality assurance systems for malaria microscopy and RDTs at the facility, sub-county, county and national levels.

Progress in the last 12 months

PMI procured 2.9 million RDTs, in addition to the 5.7 million RDTs from Global Fund, to support the launch of Kenya's nationwide roll-out of RDTs to dispensaries and health centers (i.e., levels 2 and 3) in September 2012. Prior to September 2012, PMI supported the implementation and scale-up of RDTs to 26 epidemic-prone and seasonal transmission counties in line with the NMS phased approach. By the end of 2013, PMI anticipates that an additional 4.5 million RDTs will have been procured and delivered to Kenya.

The Quality of Care survey is a nationally representative, cross-sectional survey of outpatient health facilities in Kenya. This survey is carried out twice a year and captures NMS and M&E Plan malaria case-management indicators and includes the standard PMI End Use Verification questions. The latest Quality of Care Survey, conducted in November 2012, indicated initial progress in the availability of RDTs nationally. At baseline in early 2010, 8% of health facilities had RDTs and 55% had any malaria diagnostics. By November 2012, 31% of health facilities had RDTs and 76% had any malaria diagnostics.

As part of the national implementation of RDTs, PMI supported the training of more than 3,000 health workers on RDT use, the development and dissemination of 5,000 job aides to facilities, the development of updated reporting tools that included RDTs and printing and dissemination of 4,500 reporting forms for health facilities. Testing of patients with fever and suspected malaria increased from 24% at baseline in 2010 to 47% in late 2012, based on Quality of Care survey results.

The DOMC's quality assurance plan for malaria diagnostics, which was developed with support from DFID and WHO, was operationalized on a limited scale in 2013. Building on initial trainings in 2012, four refresher trainings for over 100 personnel, including quality assurance officers and supervisory laboratory staff at the district, provincial and national levels, were conducted and supportive supervision plans were developed by the quality assurance officers for health facilities with malaria diagnostics. Quality assurance officers conducted a baseline assessment and monthly supportive supervision visits to malaria laboratory personnel in 85 health facilities in 22 targeted counties with seasonal malaria transmission. These counties were prioritized, as they have the highest ratio of ACTs prescribed to confirmed malaria cases, indicating overprescribing and wastage of ACTs, based on data quality audits conducted by the DOMC.

Malaria diagnostic services have also benefited from integrated laboratory supervision and quality assurance systems funded primarily by PEPFAR. Health facilities providing malaria diagnostic services that had at least one quality control visit in the three months prior to the Quality of Care Survey increased for microscopy from 9% to 34% and for RDTs from 5% to 22% from baseline in 2010 to late 2012.

Challenges, Opportunities and Threats

In January 2013, Kenya lost 4.5 million RDTs procured by Global Fund as a result of a central warehouse fire, which significantly decreased national stock levels, as shown in Figure 3. The loss represented half of the total RDTs purchased by donors for 2013. PMI procured an additional 4.5 million RDTs in April 2013 to address the gap created by the loss; one million have been delivered to date and the remainder is expected by the end of 2013. Because of the fire, stockouts of RDTs are expected nationally in 2013-2014, and the national roll-out of RDTs to the community level as part of the community case management strategy will likely be delayed until at least 2015.

Figure 3. Supply of Malaria Rapid Diagnostic Tests in Months at Central Level in Kenya, April 2012–April 2013 (black line – target months of stock at central level)

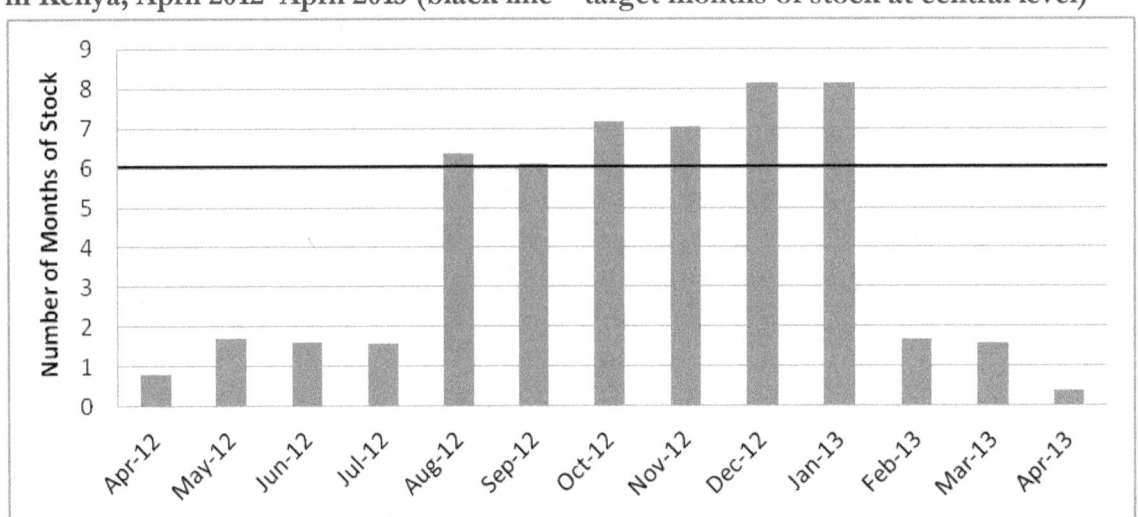

Kenya has insufficient human and financial resources to scale up the quality assurance plan for malaria diagnostics to the more than 5,000 health facilities in the country. However, with the transition to county governance, there is an opportunity to collaborate with PEPFAR to integrate supportive supervision of malaria microscopy and RDTs into broader laboratory supervision and quality assurance platforms.

Plans and Justification

In FY2014, PMI will build on the progress to date in scaling-up of malaria diagnostic testing to dispensaries and health centers nationally and scaling-up of quality assurance systems in the 26 targeted counties with epidemic-prone and seasonal malaria transmission.

The President's Malaria Initiative will procure approximately 3.75 million RDTs to help meet the projected RDT gap for national distribution to dispensaries and health centers. Table 5 shows the projected RDT needs and sources of funding from October 2013 to September 2015.

A substantial increase in funding for implementation of quality assurance systems for malaria diagnostics has been committed for FY2014 due to two primary factors: the availability of RDTs nationally at dispensaries and health centers and the transition to county governments. PMI will target quality assurance system support to 26 priority counties with epidemic-prone and seasonal transmission of malaria. Each county has a reference laboratory and approximately 100 Ministry of Health facilities with malaria diagnostic capacity. Global Fund, World Bank, DFID and WHO are also supporting implementation of the quality assurance plan for malaria diagnostics; PMI funding is intended to augment partners' efforts to reach scale at peripheral levels. Additionally, PMI will support one CDC visit to provide technical assistance for malaria diagnostics.

Table 5. Projected Rapid Diagnostic Test Needs and Sources of Funding for Kenya, October 2013–September 2015

	October 2013–September 2014	October 2014–September 2015
Projected Need	15,350,112[a]	15,350,112[a]
Sources of Funding		
Global Fund	4,910,248	9,820,492
PMI	4,500,000	3,750,000
Projected Gap	**5,939,864**	**1,779,620**
[a]Projected need is calculated by adding estimated actual consumption plus six months of buffer stock needed to ensure adequate supplies at the national level.		

Proposed Activities with FY 2014 Funding: ($2,512,000)

1. **Procure RDTs:** PMI will procure and distribute approximately 3.75 million RDTs. This will help meet the projected gap for dispensaries and health centers nationwide. *($1,500,000)*

2. **Provide supportive supervision within the established quality assurance and quality control system on malaria diagnostics:** PMI will provide technical and operational support to priority counties for operationalization, scale up and integration of quality assurance systems for malaria diagnostics. Activities in the 26 priority counties include the following (1) training and building supervisory capacity for reference laboratory staff (i.e., approximately 10) at the county level; (2) training and building supervisory capacity for a cadre of QA officers (i.e., 20–30) in each county; (3) developing work and supervisory plans; (4) facilitating baseline and quarterly supervisory and QA visits to health facilities to monitor competence for RDTs and microscopy, validate routine blood slide results, and monitor RDT storage conditions and microscopy supplies; (5) remedial and on-the-job training and mentoring for clinical and laboratory staff as necessary; and (6) monitoring and evaluation of the QA program. Each QA officer will be responsible for conducting visits to 3–5 health facilities quarterly; each reference laboratory supervisor will provide mentoring and oversight to 3–5 QA officers. Each county has an average of 100 Ministry of Health facilities offering RDTs and/or microscopy services. *($1,000,000)*

3. **Technical Assistance—CDC:** Support one CDC in-country visit to provide technical assistance for malaria diagnostics. Technical assistance will focus on working with the DOMC, National Public Health Laboratory and implementing partner to prioritize counties for operationalization and scale up of quality assurance systems and develop a schedule for deliverables and milestones. *($12,000)*

TREATMENT

DOMC/PMI Objectives

In support of Kenya's NMS of ensuring that all patients with fever presenting to a health facility receive a parasitological diagnosis through microscopy or RDT and effective treatment by 2013, PMI procures and distributes ACTs to all public health facility levels. Kenya uses AL as the first-line treatment for uncomplicated malaria and parenteral quinine, artesunate, or artemether for severe malaria.

Progress in the last 12 months

In the last year, PMI procured 3.5 million AL treatments, representing 33% of the total estimated annual AL need for Kenya. PMI contributed to maintaining consistent national ACT stocks, complementing the Global Fund ACT procurement cycles. PMI also continued to strengthen the in-country supply chain system to ensure an uninterrupted supply of ACTs to all public health facilities. Figure 4 shows stocks available at the central level from April 2012 through April 2013. Kenya has not experienced a stock out at the central level for more than two years, which is an improvement over previous years when nationwide stock outs occurred regularly. At the health facility level, the latest Quality of Care data from November 2012 shows that 92% of facilities had at least one AL weight band in stock and 72% of facilities had all AL weight bands in stock on the day of the survey.

Figure 4. Monthly Trend of ACT Stocks at the Central Level in Kenya, April 2012–April 2013 (blue bar – total months of ACTs available; black line – target months of stock at central level)

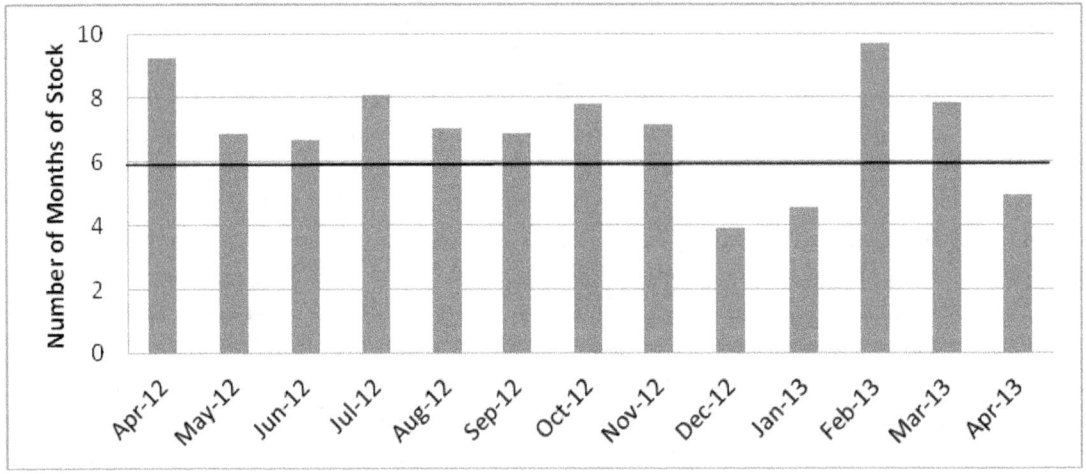

An increasing percentage of malaria test-positive patients now receive appropriate drug treatment. As measured by the Quality of Care Surveys, in clinics where both malaria diagnostics and ACTs were available, the percentage of test-positive patients treated appropriately increased from a baseline of 83% in 2010 to 92% in late 2012. In addition, the percentage of patients who received antimalarial treatment despite testing negative for malaria fell from 52% to 20% over the same period. Figure 5 demonstrates the dramatic reduction in ACT use that has occurred as RDT availability increased in health facilities between March 2012 and March 2013 as more providers adhere to the national treatment guidelines and treat only test-positive patients with an ACT. Although there is still much progress to be made, this is an encouraging trend.

Figure 5. Monthly Artemisinin-based Combination Therapy Consumption over Time, Before and After National Rapid Diagnostic Test Distribution, in Kenya from the Health Information System, March 2012–March 2013 (Black line – trend of ACT doses consumed over time)

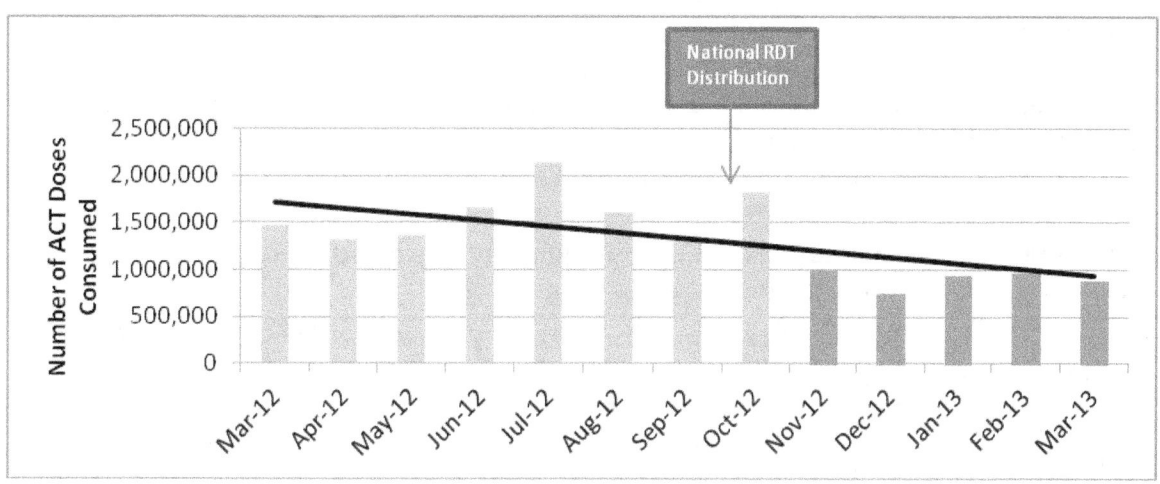

Training and supervision for malaria case management was supported nationally by Global Fund in 2012-2013; more than 3,000 health workers were trained on malaria case management and RDT use. PMI support was initially targeted to healthcare workers at the community, health-facility and sub-county levels in priority endemic counties. The DOMC and PMI were able to take advantage of significant PEPFAR resources for improving quality of healthcare services; malaria-specific support is provided through the project to communities, health facilities and sub-counties in the targeted counties. In the past year, activities in targeted counties included 1) dissemination of the national malaria strategy guidelines and supervisory checklist to 71 malaria control coordinators, 2) formation of technical working groups coordinated by the malaria control coordinators, 3) training of more than 500 healthcare providers on malaria case management, 4) training of 72 providers on RDT use and 5) training of almost 700 CHWs on malaria prevention and control. Community units in Siaya and Bungoma counties implemented malaria community case management activities. With the assistance of new training materials and increased knowledge among healthcare providers, CHWs and CHEWs, community units are now prioritizing malaria prevention during community meetings and health dialogue and action days.

Improvements in case management have occurred in the setting of increased healthcare worker in-service training and supervision provided by support from both PMI and other partners. Based on data from the Quality of Care Surveys, the percentage of healthcare workers who had received malaria-specific supervision increased from 18% at baseline to 43% in late 2012. In the three months preceding the latest survey, 79% of facilities had received at least one supervisory visit and 56% had received at least one visit that included a malaria case-management topic.

Challenges, Opportunities and Threats

The key challenges are related to devolution and national roll-out of the community case management strategy. The Global Fund supports the implementation of malaria community case management through community units and community-based organizations; however, because of RDT shortages (see Diagnosis section) and delays in scaling up functional community units, the DOMC targets have not been met to date. Scaling up community units to counties outside of the initial focus areas will require political commitment and substantial human and financial resources from donors and partners.

Plans and Justification

PMI supports biannual national quantifications to ensure that AL requirements are properly forecasted. Table 6 shows that Global Fund support is not yet assured to cover 100% of the anticipated ACT needs for the public sector. PMI support will help meet the gap as currently projected in public sector needs for ACTs in FY 2014.

Table 6. Projected Artemisinin-based Combination Therapy Needs and Sources of Funding for Kenya, October 2013–September 2015

	October 2013–September 2014	October 2014–September 2015
Projected Need	16,037,478[a]	16,037,478[a,b]
Sources of Funding		
Global Fund	4,394,800	7,166,000
PMI	5,781,062	4,800,000
Projected Gap	**5,861,616**	**4,071,478**

[a]Projected need is calculated by adding estimated actual consumption plus six months of buffer stock needed to ensure adequate supplies at the national level.
[b]Based on 2012–2013 quantification; figures are likely to change for 2014–2015 based on quantification in July 2013.

Proposed Activities with FY 2014 Funding: *($6,335,000)*

1. **Procure and distribute ACTs and/or severe malaria medication:** PMI will procure and distribute approximately 4.8 million AL treatments which will help meet the gap for ACTs in the public sector through September 2015. Severe malaria medication may be procured as needed. *($5,535,000)*

2. **Strengthen supervision and mentorship for malaria case management and prevention:** PMI will support malaria case management strengthening activities from the community to county levels in targeted endemic counties in western Kenya where the burden of malaria is concentrated. Activities at the community level include initial and refresher trainings for CHWs and CHEWs on prevention, early diagnosis, treatment, and referral, facilitating supervisory visits by CHEWs and strengthening reporting systems. Health-facility level efforts will focus on both initial and refresher malaria case management training for clinical staff, provision of job aids, supervision and mentoring of CHEWs and strengthening reporting systems. At the county level, activities include building capacity for supervision, mentoring and data use for decision making, facilitating malaria technical

working groups, and supporting supervisory visits to health facilities and community units and on-the-job training. *($600,000)*

3. *In vivo* **drug efficacy monitoring:** Support drug efficacy monitoring of current first- and second-line antimalarial medications, using the standard WHO protocol, at two sites in western Kenya. *(This activity is budgeted under the M&E section.)*

4. **Stockpile epidemic response supplies:** PMI will support the procurement of RDTs, ACTs, and potentially ITNs, for a "virtual" stockpile for epidemic response. Supplies will be held centrally and those not used for epidemic response will be recycled through routine distribution channels to avoid expiry. *($200,000)*

PHARMACEUTICAL MANAGEMENT

DOMC/PMI Objectives
In line with the Kenya NMS, PMI has supported supply chain management activities from the national to health-facility levels to ensure all Ministry of Health facilities have RDTs and all weight-based packs of ACTs, thereby preventing stock outs of essential malaria commodities

Progress in the last 12 months
PMI supported strengthening of commodity management at the national (Figures 3 and 4 in Diagnosis and Treatment sections) and subnational (i.e. provincial and sub-county) levels to ensure data were available and used to forecast and quantify commodity needs biannually, monitor the commodity pipeline and plan procurements to prevent stock outs at the central and facility levels. Pipeline monitoring informed PMI's decision to procure 3.5 million doses of AL ahead of the usual procurement cycle to avert an anticipated stock out in mid-2013. At subnational levels, PMI supported initial commodity management orientations for 350 staff, supportive supervision at over 550 health facilities in 18 sub-counties, and capacity building within regional health management teams for supply chain management and commodity security. The availability of AL at sampled health facilities has improved in the last year; 90% of sampled health facilities consistently had one or more of the four AL weight-specific presentations available since October 2012.

Historically, the DOMC, PMI, and other partners relied on the Logistics Management Information System to track malaria commodities data. The Logistic Management Information System did not produce timely data at the national level and on average, only 40% (range 37–45%) of health facilities reported data each month between January–September 2012. Therefore, the DOMC, with PMI support, integrated a malaria commodity reporting tool, which includes RDTs and ACTs, into the routine Kenya Health Information System platform to ensure all malaria indicator data was reported monthly in a single system. To facilitate the transition to malaria commodities reporting via the routine DHIS2, sub-county pharmacists actively collected data from non-reporting health facilities via telephone, short message service or visits and entered the data into the system. Reporting of malaria commodities data by health facilities increased to 72% (range 71–72%) per month between January and March 2013.

In 2012-2013, PMI continued support for antimalarial medicines quality monitoring using Minilab® (i.e., a mobile mini-laboratory for rapid drug quality verification and counterfeit medicine detection supplied by Global Pharma Health Fund) testing at five sentinel sites. The activity was implemented by the National Quality Control Laboratory and provided evidence-based data on antimalarial quality for appropriate action and enforcement by the Pharmacy and Poisons Board. Round 3 of antimalarial quality monitoring was completed in 2013 and included site visits to Mombasa and Nairobi to monitor activities and Minilab® refresher training for 24 participants from the National Quality Control Laboratory and Pharmacy and Poisons Board. Among 545 antimalarial samples collected, 514 were tested using Minilab® at the five sentinel field sites, 71 were tested at the National Quality Control Laboratory and 20 were tested using compendial methods (some samples were tested using more than one method). Only two quinine sulfate samples failed compendial testing and two medications were found to be unregistered. The Pharmacy and Poisons Board took corrective actions based on these findings; a supplier of the counterfeit products was prosecuted, a pharmacist was fined and non-conforming medications were withdrawn from market. Since 2009, the number of medicines that have failed quality testing has declined dramatically.

Challenges, Opportunities and Threats

The main challenge will be providing an uninterrupted supply of malaria commodities to the health-facility and community levels in the context of devolution to 47 county governments.

Plans and Justification

PMI will add substantial financial resources in FY 2014 to develop capacity and structures for supply chain management and strategic and operational planning for 47 counties. Required central procurement and distribution of health commodities through the parastatal Kenya Medical Supplies Authority (KEMSA) has already been a contentious issue and openly challenged by county governments. PMI expects significantly increased resources will be required during the transitional period to build county capacity while at the same time supporting the current procurement and distribution system to ensure a smooth transition and prevent interruptions and stock outs in malaria commodities. PMI also expects that there will be increased requirements for commercial logistics and transportation (e.g., private courier services) to distribute malaria commodities from central and regional levels to health facilities and within counties during the transitional period to prevent health-facility level stock outs.

Proposed Activities with FY 2014 Funding: ($1,500,000)

1. **Strengthen supply chain management for malaria commodities at the national level:** PMI will provide support to the DOMC and KEMSA to strengthen supply chain management and build capacity to ensure commodities data is available and used to accurately forecast and quantify commodity needs, monitor the commodity pipeline and plan procurements to mitigate delays in Global Fund cycles and prevent stockouts at all levels of the health system. Areas of technical and operational support to KEMSA will include warehousing, financial management, information systems and monitoring and evaluation of performance. With the transition to a "pull" distribution system and the potential for counties to use alternative pharmaceutical commodity distribution systems, on-time order delivery performance will be increasingly important for KEMSA. The DOMC and PMI are committed to working within the GoK structures and systems and optimizing performance. PMI will continue to support End Use Verification surveys (budgeted under the M&E

section) as part of the larger Quality of Care surveys conducted biannually to ensure malaria commodities are reaching intended beneficiaries. *($300,000)*.

2. **Strengthen supply chain management for malaria commodities at the county, sub-county and health-facility levels:** PMI will provide support throughout the supply chain to build capacity and structures to ensure data is available and used to quantify commodity needs and plan orders to prevent stock outs in priority endemic and seasonal transmission counties. Operational and technical activities will focus on improving the organization, management and security of commodities within regional and county warehouses, strengthening and managing county systems to order, track, and evaluate commodity distribution from KEMSA and transfer/redistribute commodities to alleviate supply shortages and avoid expiries, and troubleshooting to identify distribution bottlenecks and gaps. Capacity-building activities at the county level will focus on health management teams and pharmacists and will include training and mentoring to strengthen supervisory and decision-making skills, developing and monitoring work plans and supporting supervisory visits to sub-county health units and health facilities. To improve malaria commodity consumption data reporting via the routine health information system, PMI will support commodity management and reporting system orientations and reporting forms and job aids dissemination to health-facility, sub-county and county levels. *($900,000)*

3. **Strengthen antimalarial drug quality monitoring and surveillance:** PMI will provide technical, strategic and operational support to strengthen and expand antimalarial drug quality monitoring at the national and county levels. *($300,000)*

Monitoring & Evaluation

DOMC/PMI Objectives

The DOMC's goal is "to strengthen surveillance, monitoring and evaluation systems so that key malaria indicators are routinely monitored and evaluated in all malarious districts by 2011 through capacity strengthening for malaria surveillance, routine monitoring and operational research."

Since 2009, the DOMC and stakeholders have relied on a comprehensive national M&E Plan to enable transparent and objective monitoring and evaluation of malaria control activities. The costed M&E Plan is used for M&E advocacy, communications and resource mobilization. Kenya has a large number of stakeholders, including government, universities, research institutions, private sector, non-government organizations and donor agencies, organized into a Surveillance and M&E working group and an Operational Research working group to provide a forum for discussion and dissemination of findings of the DOMC's M&E and operational research activities.

It is expected that the upcoming midterm review of the NMS will inform a significant revision to accommodate Kenya's new administrative structures. Based on the revisions made to the national strategy, it is anticipated that an updated plan for monitoring and evaluation activities at both the national and county levels will follow shortly after. Coordinated by the DOMC, the PMI-supported impact evaluation scheduled for 2014 will build on previous studies to evaluate the impact of the malaria control interventions being scaled up in Kenya. Table 7 summarizes the available data sources and assessments in Kenya since 2007 and planned activities through 2015.

Table 7. Timeline of Data Collection Activities in Kenya, 2007–2015

Data Source	Year								
	2007	2008	2009	2010	2011	2012	2013	2014	2015
National Household Surveys									
DHS		X					X		
MICS		Xª							
MIS	Xª			X				X	
Other Surveys									
Service Provision Assessment				X					
EUV/Quality of Care[b]			X	X	X	X	X	X	X
ITN Post-Campaign Survey						X			
ITN Post-Campaign Qualitative Assessment							X		
Malaria Surveillance & Routine Health Information									
Kenya Health Information System (HIS)[c]	X	X	X	X	X	X	X	X	X
Integrated Disease Surveillance and Response	X	X	X	X	X	X	X	X	X
Health Facility Surveillance[d]							X	X	X
Sentinel surveillance in epidemic-prone districts	X	X	X	X	X	X	X	X	X
Other Data Sources and Evaluations									
PMI Impact Evaluation								X	
Rapid Epidemic Preparedness & Response assessment						X			
Malaria Program Review			X					X	
Epidemiologic Risk Map & County Malaria Profiles							X		X
World Bank Report[e]						X			
M/DHS Mortality Analysis[f]						X			
KEMRI/CDC HDSS (Kisumu)[g]	X	X	X	X	X	X	X	X	X
KEMRI/Walter Reed Project HDSS (Kisumu West)[g]					X	X	X	X	X
KEMRI/Wellcome Trust Malaria *Pf*PR$_{2\text{-}10}$ Dataset[h]	X	X	X	X	X	X	X	X	X

[a]The 2007 MIS and 2008 MICS were subnational.

[b]EUV started in 2009 and was incorporated into the Quality of Care survey in 2010.

[c]The DHIS2 platform started in 2010 to provide improved district-level facility data collection.

[d]Health facility-based surveillance in IRS districts, PMI funded. August 2012-July 2015.

[e]What has driven the infant mortality decline in Kenya? G. Demombynes and S.K. Trommlerová. *The World Bank. Policy Research Working Paper 6057.* May 2012.

[f]Report titled: Determinants of Childhood Mortality in Kenya 1998-2008/09. MEASURE DHS. December 2012.

Progress in the last 12 months

PMI supported the strengthening and implementation of a national surveillance roll-out plan based on WHO surveillance guidance. One of the initial steps included a stakeholders' workshop to develop a malaria surveillance curriculum package. The surveillance curriculum will be used to train healthcare workers on malaria surveillance, including threshold setting in epidemic-prone areas. PMI is supporting the development of the curriculum and PMI and Global Fund will support the training costs. A quarterly malaria surveillance bulletin was developed and is distributed by the DOMC to malaria stakeholders in Kenya. The bulletins include the malaria indicators recommended by the WHO surveillance guidance, standardized graphs and updates on key activities.

The DOMC, with support from PMI, conducted a rapid assessment of the implementation of the epidemic preparedness and response system in the epidemic-prone counties to identify the strengths and weaknesses of the system. Based on the assessment's recommendations, PMI will target its funding to help enhance the system as part of the overall strengthening of malaria surveillance. PMI provided support to strengthen routine malaria-specific reporting in the Health Information System's new DHIS2 platform to ensure malaria indicators were included in the reporting modules. Standard malaria indicators are reported at the facility and sub-county level on a monthly basis. The DHIS2 has proven to be extremely useful to the DOMC within the past year of operations, and the opportunity to ensure the DOMC can be part of the Health Information System/DHIS2 decision-making process is critical to the program. As mentioned in the case management section, over the past year, the DOMC, with PMI support, designed and integrated a malaria commodity reporting tool into the DHIS2 to ensure all malaria indicator data were reported monthly in a single system, which has increased the proportion of health facilities reporting on malaria commodities from 40% in 2012 to more than 70% in 2013.

A reanalysis of the 1998, 2003 and 2008-09 DHS survey data to assess determinants of childhood mortality in Kenya captured in these surveys was completed and the results are described in the Other Relevant Evidence of Progress section above. This analysis will be incorporated into the malaria impact evaluation scheduled for 2014.

Epidemiologic health facility-based surveillance in IRS sub-counties (four IRS sub-counties and one non-IRS sub-county, two facilities per sub-county) began in August 2012 with PMI support. Data will be collected over a period of 36 months, and will end in July 2015. Data is collected on suspected malaria cases, RDT test-positivity rate, and the proportion of confirmed cases prescribed an ACT. Between February-April 2013, the testing rate of suspected cases ranged from 88%-100%. The RDT test-positivity rate in children under five years of age in April 2013 (prior to peak transmission) ranged from 24%-56% in the five sub-counties. A quarterly bulletin is being developed to report the findings from this activity to the DOMC, PMI and stakeholders. Retrospective data has been collected from the ten facilities and is being analyzed to provide historic trends in outpatient malaria cases and malaria slide-positivity rates. Discussions are underway between additional donors and the DOMC regarding M&E activities surrounding IRS in western Kenya. These epidemiologic surveillance activities will build off the activities currently supported by PMI and the PMI team will remain engaged in these discussions.

PMI continued to support the Quality of Care Survey which is conducted on a semi-annual basis and incorporates PMI's standard End Use Verification indicators. The data from the Quality of Care surveys are referenced frequently to demonstrate program progress and performance. The sixth survey was conducted in June 2013 (results are not yet available).

PMI contributed to the development of an epidemiological risk report and county malaria profiles. The profiles will be updated every two years and the first round was released in 2013. The profiles include information on malaria epidemiology (e.g., predicted *Plasmodium falciparum* parasitemia rate), malaria intervention coverage and intervention coverage gaps; the county profiles are advocacy and planning tools for use by the new county governments.

PMI expanded the DOMC's capacity over the past year by providing technical assistance for its M&E and governance structures including the M&E working group and Operational Research working group. Additionally, PMI funded two DOMC focal points to attend the MEASURE Evaluation/University of Ghana Regional Workshop on Malaria M&E.

PMI supported the development of the DOMC's first annual malaria report for the fiscal year 2011-2012. PMI also supported the production of a report on supportive supervision for malaria control activities, including a summary of the supportive supervision tools and findings from the supervision visits at the health facility, district and provincial levels. The malaria supportive supervision check list was programmed into PDAs for supervision visits.

Challenges, Opportunities and Threats

Under devolution, the DOMC will continue to be responsible for national M&E activities and policy formulation; however, it is anticipated that each county will be developing their own malaria M&E plans. A critical challenge will be to determine the county-level needs and to provide them with appropriate M&E support. Human resources will become a major challenge as many counties are unlikely to have individuals trained in M&E and surveillance.

One major opportunity for PMI is to work with and leverage the support of other health programs, particularly PEPFAR, in continuing to strengthen the DHIS2 platform. A strong reporting platform will provide timely malaria data for use by the DOMC, county governments and partners to inform malaria program decisions.

Plans and Justification

The DOMC implements most malaria M&E activities through funding from the Global Fund, PMI and DFID. Available funding is targeted towards achieving:

1. Improved functioning of M&E unit resources (technical capacity, hardware and software capability, and information collection, analysis, reporting and dissemination);
2. Coordination of malaria M&E activities within the country;
3. Improved data flow to/from all levels of the healthcare system;
4. Data quality assurance; and,
5. Using data for decision making.

With FY 2014 funding, PMI will continue to support the implementation of the national malaria M&E Plan. PMI will work with the DOMC and partners to ensure continuity of M&E and surveillance activities and will work to identify areas of support for malaria M&E activities at the county level. There has been a renewed effort to strengthen the malaria surveillance system in Kenya, and PMI will be supporting this along with other partners. PMI will continue to work with WHO, Global Fund, DFID and other malaria partners in support of M&E and surveillance activities in Kenya.

Proposed PMI Activities with FY 2014 Funding: *($1,062,000)*

1. **Support the implementation of national and county M&E Plans:** Continue support for implementation of the national M&E plan by providing technical assistance to increase the capacity of existing DOMC M&E staff and new county malaria M&E staff to ensure that data is used for program improvements. Specific activities are listed below. *($500,000)*
   - Support the DOMC in revision of the M&E Plan following the mid-term review of the NMS in 2014
   - Support priority counties to develop M&E plans, as needed
   - Provide technical assistance to the DOMC for follow-up activities to the 2014 MIS, including review of the estimates, report writing and dissemination activities
   - Provide support for updating the county malaria profiles in 2015
   - Support the DOMC in analysis and presentation of data for quarterly surveillance bulletins, annual malaria reports, briefs for policy makers, and updates on the DOMC website
   - Support M&E training for DOMC and county malaria staff

2. **Strengthen the malaria surveillance system:** Provide support for the strengthening of routine malaria surveillance systems. The malaria surveillance system is intended to cover all counties and all health facilities utilizing reporting through DHIS2. Starting in 2013, the DOMC, with support from PMI and other donors, will expand surveillance training beyond the highlands of western Kenya to the epidemic areas of the arid and semi-arid lands and eventually nationally. FY 2014 funds will be used to provide continued support for the roll-out of the national surveillance strategy. Specifically, FY 2014 funding will help the DOMC monitor malaria indicators, train healthcare workers on malaria surveillance in all epidemiologic zones, train healthcare workers and county and sub-county malaria focal persons in epidemic-prone counties on threshold setting, create and distribute surveillance job aides, and support reporting and response activities. *($200,000)*

3. **Strengthen the health information system and the collection of information at the health facility and county levels:** The Kenya Health Information System via the DHIS2 platform collects routine data at the health-facility level. The DOMC is heavily reliant on the integrated DHIS2 platform to collect routine health-facility level data since it uses the health systems that are already in place to collect routine data. The $32.8 million, five-year project is funded primarily through PEPFAR. PMI and the DOMC will leverage this funding and take advantage of the ongoing investment in improving the DHIS2 to collect additional malaria

data at the health-facility, sub-county and county levels to allow for informed decision making for malaria programs at the national and county levels. *($200,000)*

4. **Monitoring of interventions:** Support M&E activities for specific intervention areas: *($150,000)*
   a. *End-Use Verification tool/Quality of Care Survey:* Monitor stocks of ACTs and RDTs through the End Use Verification tool. The data collection will be done semiannually as part of the DOMC's Quality of Care survey to allow for a comprehensive evaluation of case management progress and performance. Approximately 170 of the 5713 health facilities will be randomly sampled each time, for a total of 340 health facilities sampled per year. The nationally representative sample includes dispensaries, health centers and hospitals owned by the GoK, faith-based organizations and NGOs across the country, excluding Nairobi. Global Fund provides the majority of funding for this activity. *($100,000)*

   b. In vivo *drug efficacy monitoring:* Support drug efficacy monitoring, using the standard WHO protocol, at two sites in western Kenya. *($50,000)*

5. **Technical assistance—CDC:** Support one CDC in-country visit to provide technical assistance for M&E activities. *($12,000)*

Behavior Change Communication

DOMC/PMI Objectives

The objective of the NMS is to strengthen advocacy, communication and social mobilization capacities for malaria control to ensure that at least 80% of people in malarious areas have knowledge of malaria prevention and treatment measures by 2014. To achieve this objective, the DOMC developed a communication strategy in 2010 to guide and inform message development for malaria control interventions. The process of developing the communication strategy involved consultations with multiple stakeholders in the private and public sectors as well as development partners.

The strategy delineates the various primary and secondary stakeholders, their information needs and recommends messages and communication channels, tools and tactics that should be used to reach them and ensure positive behavior change that will eventually lead to the realization of the objectives. In 2012, the DOMC and its partners, with support from PMI, also developed an Essential Malaria Action Guide for Kenyan Families, which outlines key actions and messages for each intervention area to ensure that all partners and stakeholders involved in malaria control are disseminating the same messages and taking appropriate actions. This guide was developed in accordance with the Rollback Malaria Partnership's Strategic Framework for Malaria Communication at the Country Level, 2012-2017. The Essential Malaria Action Guide has sections covering use of ITNs, IRS, case management and MIP prevention.

Progress in the last 12 months

In the last year, PMI continued support for behavior change communication activities both at the national and community levels. The promotional activities focused on ensuring that the highest-risk groups are aware of, have access to and consistently use the available malaria control tools. In 2013, PMI continued support to targeted malaria-endemic counties.

In these targeted counties, PMI funded intensive community-based interventions through interpersonal communication at the household level in three districts with very high malaria morbidity. The CHWs visited 81,083 households; they found 156,802 nets, of which 16,178 (10%) had not been hung. The CHWs assisted in hanging 11,446 of these nets and also gave information on the importance of consistently using nets. The CHWs also carried out other promotional activities though *barazas* (i.e., community meetings organized by the area chief or administrator) where they discussed the importance of prompt and appropriate treatment for malaria and of attendance at ANC clinics for pregnant women to access ITNs and IPTp for malaria prevention.

At the national level, PMI supported the development of advocacy materials on the appropriate use of RDTs as part of the launch and roll out of 8.6 million RDTs in the public sector (as discussed in the case management section, above). These information and education materials will help to ensure proper diagnosis of malaria before treatment in accordance with national case management guidelines, which will promote the rational use of ACTs and deter the development of resistance.

PMI/Kenya has partnered with Peace Corps since FY 2011 in malaria activities. PMI supported three Peace Corps-recruited malaria volunteers in 2012-2013. The three malaria volunteers worked closely with the DOMC, district malaria control coordinators, CHEWs, CHWs and other stakeholders to support community-based malaria control activities. The malaria volunteers were based in villages located in the three malaria-endemic regions of Kenya.

In schools, the malaria volunteers taught pupils the cause of malaria and actions that they can take to prevent malaria. At the household level, the malaria volunteers conducted follow-up visits to pregnant women to track ANC attendance and adherence to malaria prevention including IPTp2 and ITN use. At the community level, the malaria volunteers hosted talks on malaria prevention and control using the Essential Malaria Guide and held sessions on ITN use, care and repair. For World Malaria Day 2013, the malaria volunteers recruited more than 70 Peace Corps volunteers across Kenya to host malaria-themed community activities such as football tournaments, song and drama performances, movie screenings, ITN sales, educational talks and demonstrations of ITN hanging, washing and repairs that attracted over 10,000 participants from local communities.

Challenges, Opportunities and Threats

After the mass net distribution in 2012, the DOMC carried out an evaluation to determine net use and coverage. The evaluation results indicated that net ownership with one net increased to 83.3%, while 67.1% of all households owned more than one net, however net use was still low with only 22.7% of children under five sleeping under a net and 31.9% of the general population sleeping under a net. As a results of this finding the community-strategy approach, which is being supported by the GoK, provides an opportunity for CHWs to use interpersonal communication skills to ensure that ITNs are consistently used by at-risk groups at the household level. Community health workers will engage with household members at a personal level during household visits to assess the health needs of families. During these visits the CHWs will be able to discuss at length the reasons for not using ITNs consistently and any other health practices that promote positive health behaviors. Interpersonal communication, when carried out correctly, is very effective in encouraging behavior change in care seekers. Behavior change communication, like any other intervention, will be affected by the devolution process and all other partners are following the process closely to ensure that the existing BCC working group remains responsive to the new management structure and realigns itself to meet new challenges.

Plans and Justification

In FY 2014 malaria information, education and communication (IEC) and BCC activities will be more focused at the community level where the community strategy will provide a platform for getting malaria control messages to at risk groups using interpersonal communication to ensure discussions on the importance of malaria control through the available control tools. Other channels of communication will also be used to ensure that other target groups are also reached with messages through radio spots, television and print media.

Proposed PMI Activities with FY 2014 Funding: ($1,030,000)

With FY 2014 funding, PMI will continue to support IEC/BCC activities. Specific activities include:

1. **Integrated community-based IEC/BCC:** Expand community-based IEC/BCC efforts by increasing outreach to priority populations in endemic and epidemic-prone districts, especially pregnant women and children under five years of age, through different strategies and channels of communication. Increased interpersonal communication delivered via the community approach will be one of the main channels of communication at the household level, which will ensure that there is enough discussion between community health workers and household heads on the use of the various malaria control tools available. In addition, messages and modes of dissemination will be dependent on the venue and target group. In health facilities and antenatal clinics, health talks and interpersonal communication during consultation will be used as well as posters depicting the various health practices needed for the prevention of malaria, while *barazas* will be held in villages and during public gatherings where messages will be delivered through public address systems. During these sessions, skits and dramas will be used to deliver messages on malaria control in a more engaging manner in order to:
   - Increase ITN ownership and promote correct and consistent use of ITNs;
   - Promote early and regular ANC attendance by pregnant women to increase the proportion of women using IPTp;
   - Increase early and appropriate health-seeking behavior and prompt diagnosis for all persons with fever. *($900,000)*

2. **National IEC/BCC promotion and material production:** It will be necessary to support national IEC/BCC efforts to ensure that all 47 counties are cognizant of the national IEC/BCC strategies, polices and guidelines on malaria control in the country. PMI will support national-level IEC message development and dissemination of key malaria control interventions related to the new policies and guidelines (i.e. MIP, case management, diagnosis, IRS, etc.). The DOMC will work with partners to roll out any new messages around the control intervention areas. As RDTs continue to be rolled out in all parts of the country, PMI will support the continued dissemination of IEC materials with information on RDTs. To ensure that malaria control remains a national priority, PMI will work with other partners and coordinate donors to undertake advocacy-related activities, including regular

review meetings to monitor and guide their progress in malaria control interventions. *($100,000)*

3. **Peace Corps support:** Under the PMI-Peace Corps Initiative, continue to support three Malaria Support Volunteers who will work under the guidance of PMI country advisors and the host government and other stakeholders to support malaria control activities at the county level where they will work with the County Malaria Control Coordinators. The Peace Corps volunteers will provide technical support to community-based groups working in malaria control interventions at the county level. PMI will support these three Peace Corps volunteers with resources to carry out BCC activities around any of the intervention areas namely - IRS, ITNs, MIP and case management, as well as in cross-cutting areas of capacity building, monitoring, evaluation, and operations research, as identified by the respective County Health Management Teams. *($30,000)*

Capacity Building and Health Systems Strengthening

DOMC/PMI Objectives
An objective of the DOMC is to strengthen the capacity of technical officers and teams through human resource and infrastructure development in order to achieve the overall objectives of the NMS at all levels of the health care system. The DOMC, with support from development partners, strives to ensure that its technical and managerial personnel have the relevant skill sets to manage the different malaria control interventions by providing training opportunities for them to acquire these skills needed skills. The DOMC currently has 24 staff members at the national level. It is expected that by the end of 2013, the national level DOMC staffing numbers will also be reduced with several being transferred to key counties.

Progress in the last 12 months
Capacity Building
Recent PMI support to the DOMC has centered on building supervisory and management capacity and providing resources for supportive supervision from the national to sub-national levels to ensure program was meeting targets and milestones for progress and performance. Building on work in previous years in M&E capacity building, PMI supported the training of ten DOMC staff for a senior management and leadership course sponsored by the Kenya Institute of Administration. PMI also supported training for 13 DOMC staff in quantitative and qualitative data analysis, which was implemented by MEASURE Evaluation, Tulane University, and Kenyatta University.

PMI supported the training of two Field Epidemiology and Laboratory Training Program (FELTP) residents as a step to address the human resource gap at the county level in a two-year program. The graduates are likely to play an increasingly important role as devolution proceeds. During this reporting period the FELTP residents worked with the DOMC to complete a malaria outbreak investigation in Pokot North and an evaluation of the malaria surveillance system in the 45 epidemic-prone sub-counties in western Kenya. The FELTP residents are scheduled to work with two of PMI's implementing partners on an evaluation of the initial implementation of quality assurance for malaria diagnostics and a MIP knowledge, attitudes and practices study beginning in mid-2013.

Contributions to Health System Strengthening

PMI strengthens the overall health system by improving governance in the pharmaceutical sector, strengthening pharmaceutical management systems, expanding access to essential malaria commodities nationwide, improving health services delivery, implementing quality assurance systems for diagnostics and providing training and supervision at all levels of the system. Over the past year, PMI provided support to the DOMC to enable them to design a reporting form for malaria commodities at the facility level in the DHIS2 data collection menu and thus, providing a routine method to collect data on malaria commodities indicators and inform the quantification of RDTs and ACTs. PMI has continued its support to commodity management and quality monitoring through the Logistics Management Information System and drug quality monitoring at selected sentinel sites. PMI also supported the strengthening of routine malaria surveillance at the health-facility level through the development of a national malaria surveillance curriculum based on WHO surveillance guidance; the DOMC is now implementing initial training for the nationwide rollout of the malaria surveillance curriculum to all health facilities in late 2013.

Challenges, Opportunities and Threats

The new county health structures are likely to put pressure on the staffing patterns, particularly at the national level. The transfer of personnel from the national level to the counties has already started. Loss of key technical officers will place additional responsibilities on personnel remaining at the national level, which will likely require task shifting and an expanded scope of work. Additional challenges include the loss of an FELTP-trained mentor/supervisor at the DOMC this past year and now with the potential for downsizing of personnel at the DOMC there will be fewer people available to mentor/supervise FELTP residents. As a result of these changes, the DOMC, PMI/Kenya team and FELTP program have decided to train one FELTP resident per year rather than two.

However, if devolution is successfully implemented, there is also potential for increased stability within the health system at the county level. Counties will have the ability to retain trained personnel unlike in the previous system, in which the national government often transferred personnel with impunity.

Plans and Justification

PMI, in collaboration with Global Fund and other partners, will continue to support the DOMC in building technical and managerial capacity for staff both at the national and county levels to ensure that the program meets its core functions in line with the NMS.

Proposed PMI Activities with FY 2014 Funding: ($610,000)

With the FY 2014 funding, PMI will continue to support the DOMC to ensure that it has the technical and managerial capacity to carry out its core functions under the new devolved government (some health systems strengthening activities are incorporated into activities funded in the prior intervention areas). Specifically, PMI will fund the following:

1. **PMI direct technical support to DOMC**: Provide technical support by USAID and CDC PMI Advisors to the DOMC. The Advisors will spend a portion of their work week with the DOMC and will have a workstation within the DOMC offices to effectively integrate into the national team. (*No cost for this support*)

2. Support to DOMC: *($250,000)*
   a. *DOMC capacity building:* Improve the DOMC's technical capacity with regard to implementation and supervision. PMI's funding will enable the DOMC program management team to supervise and track malaria prevention and control activities in priority counties. The DOMC, in collaboration with county health officers, will mentor health workers in the counties and sub-counties to enhance their skills in managing malaria control interventions *($170,000)*
   b. *Attendance of DOMC staff at technical consultative meetings:* Provide assistance for DOMC program management team members and priority county malaria control coordinators to attend key technical meetings (e.g., East Africa Regional Laboratory Network conference). Attendees will be expected to make presentations and share key technical updates with technical working groups and stakeholders. *($50,000)*
   c. *Support to technical working groups:* As essential teams that review and update guidelines and changes in malaria control interventions and approaches, the DOMC will develop new approaches to realign the existing technical working groups to fit with the new administrative structures established at the national and county levels to ensure that technical and policy issues about malaria control interventions are addressed and responded to appropriately and in a timely fashion. *($30,000)*

3. **Support for new county malaria control programs**: PMI will support the new county malaria control programs to develop malaria-specific work plans consistent with each county's malaria profile and the NMS and M&E Plan to ensure the delivery, coordination and continuity of malaria prevention and control activities. The county malaria control coordinators will be expected to provide critical links with the DOMC and to ensure that the national program is kept apprised of all malaria control activities at the county. It is expected that by 2014, PMI will be supporting the county administrative structures directly through existing partnerships to ensure support at the county level, beyond technical assistance. *($300,000)*

4. **Support FELTP:** Provide support to train one malaria FELTP resident for the full two-year training program. FELTP graduates are likely to play an increasingly important role as devolution proceeds and staff trained in epidemiology are needed at the county level. The budget for each trainee includes tuition, stipend, laptop, materials, training, travel, and conferences for the two-year program. *($60,000)*

Staffing & Administration

Two health professionals serve as Resident Advisors to oversee PMI in Kenya, one representing CDC and one representing USAID. In addition, a full-time FSN works as part of the PMI team. All PMI staff members are part of a single interagency team led by the USAID Mission Director or his/her designee in country. The PMI team shares responsibility for development and implementation of PMI strategies and work plans, coordination with national authorities, managing collaborating agencies and supervising day-to-day activities. Candidates for Resident Advisor positions, whether initial hires or replacements, will be evaluated and/or interviewed jointly by USAID and CDC, and both agencies will be involved in hiring decisions, with the final decision made by the individual agency.

The PMI professional staff work together to oversee all technical and administrative aspects of PMI, including finalizing details of the project design, implementing malaria prevention and treatment activities, monitoring and evaluation of outcomes and impact, reporting of results, and providing guidance to PMI partners.

The PMI lead in country is the USAID Mission Director. The two PMI Resident Advisors, one from USAID and one from CDC, report to the Senior USAID Health Officer for day-to-day leadership, and work together as a part of a single interagency team. The technical expertise housed in Atlanta, GA and Washington, DC guides PMI programmatic efforts, and thus, overall technical guidance for both Resident Advisors falls to the PMI headquarters staff. Since CDC Resident Advisors are CDC employees (CDC USDD—38), responsibility for completing official performance reviews lies with the CDC Country Director who is expected to rely upon input from PMI staff across the two agencies that work closely with the CDC Resident Advisor and thus are best positioned to comment on the Resident Advisor's performance.

The two PMI Resident Advisors are based within the USAID health office and are expected to spend approximately half their time sitting with and providing technical assistance to the national malaria control programs and partners.

Locally-hired staff to support PMI activities either in Ministries or in USAID will be approved by the USAID Mission Director. Because of the need to adhere to specific country policies and USAID accounting regulations, any transfer of PMI funds directly to Ministries or host governments will require approval by the USAID Mission Director and Controller, in addition to the PMI Coordinator.

Proposed PMI Activities with FY 2014 Funding: ($1,665,000)

1. **USAID in-country administration and staffing:** Support for one PMI and one FSN staff members to oversee activities supported by PMI in Kenya. Additionally, these funds will support pooled USAID Kenya Mission staff and mission-wide assistance from which PMI benefits. *($1,100,000)*

2. **CDC in-country administration and staffing:** Support for one PMI staff member to oversee activities supported by PMI in Kenya. Additionally, these funds will support pooled USAID Kenya Mission staff and mission-wide assistance from which PMI benefits. *($565,000)*

Table 1: Year 7 (FY 2014) Budget Breakdown by Partner

Partner Organization	Geographic Area	Activity Description	Activity Budget	Partner Subtotals
Afya Info	Nationwide	Strengthen the Health Information System and the collection of information at the health facility and county level	$200,000	$200,000
APHIA Plus HCM	Targeted Endemic Counties	Logistic and program support for ITN distribution to the routine and mass campaign activities	$1,800,000	$3,380,000
		Support Continuous Distribution Systems	$300,000	
		Integrated community-based IEC/BCC	$900,000	
	Nationwide	National IEC/BCC promotion and material production	$100,000	
		Peace Corps support	$30,000	
		Support to DOMC	$250,000	
APHIA plus "Zone 1"	Counties in western Kenya	Strengthen supervision and mentorship for malaria case management and prevention	$600,000	$600,000
CDC IAA (with sub-grant to KEMRI)	Endemic Counties	Entomological monitoring of IRS effectiveness in sprayed sub-county areas	$330,000	
CDC IAA (Atlanta)	Endemic Counties	Technical Assistance: CDC TDYs	$24,000	$438,000
		Technical Assistance: CDC TDY	$12,000	
	Nationwide	Technical Assistance: CDC TDYs	$12,000	
		Support FELTP	$60,000	
DELIVER	Endemic/Epidemic Counties	Procure and distribute ITNs for continuous distribution and the 2014—2015 mass distribution campaign	$6,550,000	$13,785,000
	Nationwide	Procure RDTs	$1,500,000	
	Nationwide	Purchase AL and/or severe malaria medication	$5,535,000	
	Targeted County(ies)	Stockpile epidemic response supplies	$200,000	

HCSM	Nationwide	Strengthen supply chain management for malaria commodities at the national level	*$300,000*	**$1,300,000**
	Targeted Counties (Endemic & Seasonal)	Strengthen supply chain management for malaria commodities at the county, sub-county and health-facility levels	*$900,000*	
	Nationwide	Monitoring of interventions: the End-Use Verification tool/Quality of Care Survey	*$100,000*	
IRS2 TO	Endemic Counties	IRS implementation and management	*$7,982,000*	**$7,982,000**
MEASURE Evaluation PIMA	Nationwide	Support the implementation of the National and County M&E plans	*$500,000*	**$700,000**
		Strengthen the malaria surveillance system	*$200,000*	
Walter Reed	Nationwide	Monitoring of interventions: In vivo drug efficacy monitoring	*$50,000*	**$50,000**
TBD	Priority Endemic Counties	Support supervision of FANC/IPTp program	*$700,000*	**$2,300,000**
		Support for new county malaria control programs	*$300,000*	
	Nationwide	Provide supportive supervision within the established quality assurance/quality control system on malaria diagnostics	*$1,000,000*	
		Strengthen antimalarial drug quality monitoring and surveillance	*$300,000*	
USAID/CDC	Nationwide	USAID and CDC in country staffing and administration	*$1,665,000*	**$1,665,000**

FY 2014 Budget Total $32,400,000

Table 2: FY 2014 Planned Obligations Kenya

PMI-Kenya FY2014 MOP
Year 7: Table 2

Proposed Activity	Mechanism	FY 2014 Budget	FY 2014 Commodities	Geographic area	Description of Activity
Indoor Residual Spraying					
IRS implementation and management	IRS2 Task Order	$7,982,000	$2,634,060	Endemic Counties	Support IRS in up to 3 endemic counties (estimated to reach 550,000 structures and up to 2 million people in each of the two rounds of IRS), in partnership with DFID, with a target of 85% coverage in all targeted areas.
Entomological monitoring of IRS effectiveness in sprayed sub-county areas	CDC IAA (with sub-grant to KEMRI)	$330,000	$0	Endemic Counties	Continue insecticide resistance monitoring in endemic counties targeted for spraying by PMI in western Kenya, entomologic monitoring will also continue in areas where IRS is withdrawn.
Technical assistance: CDC TDYs	CDC IAA (Atlanta)	$24,000	$0	Endemic Counties	Support two visits from CDC to provide assistance in implementing IRS activities.
Subtotal		**$8,336,000**	**$2,634,060**		
Insecticide Treated Nets					
Procure and distribute ITNs for continuous distribution and the 2014-2015 mass distribution campaign	DELIVER	$6,550,000	$6,550,000	Endemic/ Epidemic Counties	Fill the ITN gap for continuous distribution and the 2014/2015 mass campaign by purchasing up to 1.8 million ITNs. Routine distribution: free-of-charge to pregnant women and children under one through the ANC and child welfare care clinics. Nets are estimated at $3.60 each.
Logistic and program support for ITN distribution to the routine and mass campaign activities	APHIA Plus HCM	$1,800,000	$0	Endemic/ Epidemic Counties	Provide logistical support, including transportation and storage of nets, for distribution of the 1.8 million ITNs within the national routine distribution system.

Activity	Partner	Budget	Budget	Location	Description
Support continuous distribution systems	APHIA Plus HCM	$300,000	$0	Selected Priority Endemic Counties	Support DOMC in follow-up activities and policy development based on the community-based ITN distribution pilot. This activity will support start-up costs for adoption of this new system in the remaining counties. Activities will include: supporting a national level technical working group meeting to review the evidence of the pilot and revise national policy, training-of-trainers for county-level officials to learn and adopt the new program, and the publication of job aids and training materials to support the roll out.
Subtotal		$8,650,000	$6,550,000		
Malaria in Pregnancy					
Sensitize and train healthcare workers on MIP simplified guidelines and IPTp "memo"	TBD	$250,000	$0	Priority Endemic Counties (Bungoma & Homa Bay)	All healthcare workers and CHEWs in Homa Bay and Bugoma counties will be sensitized and oriented on MIP using the memo and simplified guidelines. An estimated total of 2,500 healthcare workers will be reached. The orientation will include the use of the Ministry of Health IPTp memo and the current simplified MIP guidelines that have been developed and produced with PMI support.
Sensitize, orientate, and supervise CHWs	TBD	$400,000	$0	Priority Endemic Counties (Bungoma & Homa Bay)	This activity will include the orientation and training of CHWs on Community Malaria in Pregnancy. CHWs are trained to undertake BCC activities and to refer and track pregnant women to ensure that they receive IPTp at health facilities. An estimated 4,000 CHWs will be sensitized and oriented using the community strategy and other innovative community approaches. The target is to reach approximately 40,000 women of reproductive age with community MIP messages and services.
Strengthen national and county level policy and monitoring capacity	TBD	$50,000	$0	Priority Endemic Counties (Bungoma & Homa Bay)	Though most of the activity implementation will be at county level, limited support will be provided at the national level in the areas of policy and monitoring of MIP-specific activities. It is also expected that technical support will be provided to counties on MIP, as necessary.
Subtotal		$700,000	$0		

Case Management

Diagnostics

Activity	Mechanism			Location	Description
Procure RDTs	DELIVER	$1,500,000	$1,500,000	Nationwide	In support of DOMC's RDT scale-up plan, procure and distribute 3,750,000 RDTs to fill the complete gap at level 2 and 3 health facilities (dispensaries and health centers) in targeted counties and to provide initial RDT support for the community case management strategy.
Provide supportive supervision within the established quality assurance/quality control system on malaria diagnostics	TBD	$1,000,000	$0	Nationwide	Support operationalization, scale up and integration of quality assurance systems for malaria diagnostics in 26 priority counties. Strengthen capacity of existing laboratory staff for malaria diagnostics through supportive supervision of county level QA officers, within the QA/QC system. Includes: initial and refresher training of QA officers and technical supervision for adherence to testing guidelines and competency for microscopy and RDTs. Monitoring of RDT storage conditions and microscopy supplies, and program monitoring and evaluation.
Technical assistance: CDC TDY	CDC IAA (Atlanta)	$12,000	$0	Nationwide	Support one CDC TDY to provide technical assistance for malaria diagnostics.
Subtotal		$2,512,000	$1,500,000		

Treatment

Activity	Mechanism			Location	Description
Purchase artemether-lumefantrine and/or severe malaria medication	DELIVER	$5,535,000	$5,535,000	Nationwide	Procure and distribute up to 4.8 million AL treatments and severe malaria drugs, as needed, to fill in supply gaps in the public sector through September 2015. Procure severe malaria drugs, injectable aretesunate, as needed.
Strengthen supervision and mentorship for malaria case management and prevention	APHIA plus "Zone 1"	$600,000	$0	Counties in western Kenya	Strengthen supervision and mentorship for malaria control interventions with the county health management teams (CHMTs) at the health facility and community levels. Activities will include promotion of prevention and treatment activities.
Stockpile epidemic response supplies	DELIVER	$200,000	$200,000	Targeted County(ies)	Support the procurement of supplies for epidemic response including; RDTs for diagnosis, ACTs and severe malaria medicines for large-scale treatment. May include ITNs if needed.
Subtotal		$6,335,000	$5,735,000		

Pharmaceutical Management

Objective	Partner	Area		Budget	Description
Strengthen supply chain management for malaria commodities at the national level	HCSM	Nationwide	$0	$300,000	Support the DOMC and KEMSA to strengthen supply chain management and build capacity to ensure commodities data are available (through DHIS2) and used to accurately forecast and quantify commodity needs at the national level and prevent stock outs at all levels of the health system. Areas of technical and operational support to KEMSA will include warehousing, financial management, information systems and monitoring and evaluation of performance.
Strengthen supply chain management for malaria commodities at the county, sub-county and health-facility levels	HCSM	Targeted Counties (Endemic & Seasonal)	$0	$900,000	Support throughout the supply chain (county, sub-county and health-facility levels) to build capacity and structures to ensure data is available and used to quantify commodity needs and plan orders to prevent stock outs. Activities will focus on improving the organization, management and security of commodities within regional and county warehouses, strengthening county systems to order, track and evaluate commodity distribution from KEMSA and transfer/redistribute commodities to alleviate supply shortages and avoid expiries. Supervision of stock monitoring, on-the-job training and collection of antimalarial drug consumption data. Assist with distributing job aids and materials to health facilities.
Strengthen antimalarial drug quality monitoring and surveillance	TBD	Nationwide	$0	$300,000	Strengthen antimalarial drug quality monitoring through the provision of technical, strategic and operational support to the PPB and DOMC.
Subtotal			**$0**	**$1,500,000**	
Monitoring & Evaluation					
Support the implementation of the National and County M&E plans	MEASURE Evaluation PIMA	Nationwide	$0	$500,000	Continue support for implementation of the national M&E plan by providing technical assistance to increase the capacity of existing DOMC M&E staff and to ensure that data is used for program improvements. Support for revision of the national M&E plan and development of county M&E plans and activities. Assist with follow-up activities for the 2014 MIS. Update county malaria profiles.

Activity	Partner	Cost	Location	Description
Strengthen the malaria surveillance system	MEASURE Evaluation PIMA	$200,000	Nationwide	Support rollout of the surveillance curriculum nationally and continuity of activities. Continue support for training healthcare workers on malaria surveillance and epidemic threshold setting. PMI will help to fill gaps in Global Fund support for surveillance. Continue with capacity building in counties, mentorship, maintenance of activities and reporting.
Strengthen the Health Information System and the collection of information at the health facility and county level	Afya Info	$200,000	Nationwide	Strengthen the malaria-specific reporting in the Health Information System's District Health Information System (DHIS2), which gathers routine data at the health facility level. Ensure malaria information is captured through the DHIS2. Continued to strengthen the malaria component of the DHIS2 system in a devolved context where M&E will remain at the national level.
Monitoring of interventions: the End-Use Verification tool/Quality of Care Survey	HCSM	$100,000	Nationwide	Monitor quality of care for malaria case management and assess stock outs through the End-Use Verification tool.
Monitoring of interventions: *In vivo* drug efficacy monitoring	Walter Reed	$50,000	Nationwide	Continue *in vivo* drug efficacy monitoring at eight established DOMC sites to test the sensitivity of AL and examine efficacy of ACTs.
Technical Assistance: CDC TDYs	CDC IAA (Atlanta)	$12,000	Nationwide	Support one CDC TDY to provide technical assistance for M&E activities.
Subtotal		**$1,062,000**		
Behavior Change and Communication		**$0**		
Integrated community-based IEC/BCC	APHIA Plus HCM	$900,000	Targeted Endemic Counties	Expand community-based IEC/BCC efforts by increasing outreach to priority population's especially pregnant women and children under five years through different strategies and channels of communication, such as IPC. Messages and mode of dissemination will be dependent on the venue and target group. In hospitals, at the ANC clinics, interpersonal communication will be used as well as in homes during home visits by community health workers, while *barazas* will be held in villages and during public gatherings where messages are delivered through public address systems.

Activity	Description	Location			Mechanism
National IEC/BCC promotion and material production	Support national-level IEC message development and dissemination on key malaria control interventions on the new policies, donor coordination, undertake advocacy-related activities, including regular review meetings with donors working in the malaria constituency to monitor and advise on their progress in malaria control interventions. Activities will help strengthen the Division of Health Promotion.	Nationwide	$0	$100,000	APHIA Plus HCM
Peace Corps support	Continue PC activities and support three malaria PCVs.	Nationwide	$0	$30,000	APHIA Plus HCM
Subtotal			**$0**	**$1,030,000**	
Capacity Building and Health Systems Strengthening					
Support to DOMC	Provision of technical assistance and capacity building to improve the DOMC's technical capacity to fulfill its role in support to implementation and mentorship; ensure the technical working groups are strengthened and hold regular meetings.	Nationwide	$0	$250,000	APHIA Plus HCM
Support for new county malaria control programs	Strengthen malaria coordinators at the county level to ensure that they are able to manage the new county-level malaria programs that need to be operationalized. Support emerging malaria control issues at the county level.	Priority Endemic Counties	$0	$300,000	TBD
Support FELTP	Train one FELTP trainee for the two-year program. Upon graduation the trainee will be seconded to the DOMC or county malaria control program to increase the long-term capacity within the country to carry out appropriate program planning, implementation and monitoring and evaluation. The budget for each trainee includes tuition, stipend, laptop, materials, training and travel for the two years.	Nationwide	$0	$60,000	CDC IAA (Atlanta)
Subtotal			**$0**	**$610,000**	
Staffing and Administration					
PMI in-country administration and staffing	USAID and CDC Staffing and Mission-wide support efforts	Nationwide	$0	$1,665,000	USAID and CDC IAA (Atlanta)
Subtotal			**$0**	**$1,665,000**	
GRAND TOTAL			**$16,419,060**	**$32,400,000**	

www.ingramcontent.com/pod-product-compliance
Lightning Source LLC
Chambersburg PA
CBHW080550290526
45790CB00006B/2614